Successful
Marketing

Eric Davies

www.inaweek.co.uk

Hodder Education

338 Euston Road, London NW1 3BH.

Hodder Education is an Hachette UK company.

First published in UK 1992 by Hodder Education

This edition published 2012.

Previous editions of this book were published by Hodder in 1992, 1998 and 2002

www.hoddereducation.co.uk

Typeset by Cenveo Publisher Services.

Printed in Great Britain by CPI Group (UK) Ltd, Croydon, CR0 4YY.

Also available
in ebook

Contents

Introduction

Marketing is about the relationship between an organization and its marketplace, and in particular its customers and potential customers. Customers are the lifeblood of a business; without customers a business has no future. In order to succeed and make a profit, a business must therefore aim to identify and satisfy the needs of its customers. The purpose of marketing is to help the business achieve these aims. In this book you will learn, in a week, about the nature and techniques of successful marketing and how it can improve business performance.

On Sunday we will consider the definition of marketing, what it is and what it is not, and the relationship between marketing and business performance. On Monday we will study the customer, their motives, values and attitudes and buyer behaviour (in customer and business-to-business markets). On Tuesday we focus on marketing information and marketing research and look at the techniques and processes used to obtain information to reduce risk in marketing decision making. Wednesday's chapter describes marketing as a strategic activity and looks at the marketing decision process, as well as some of the most famous strategic techniques including the Boston Box, the Ansoff Box and Michael Porter's Three Generic Strategies.

We spend the rest of the week looking in detail at the marketing mix – product, price, place and promotion, also known as the 4 Ps. On Thursday we consider first the product element, which covers tangible and intangible benefits, brands, the product life cycle, new product development and product strategy decisions. We also look at price, which includes customers' perceptions of value, our cost structure and competitors' prices and value offerings. On Friday we focus on place - specifically the channels of distribution that are used to make the product or service available to the customer. Finally, on Saturday we review promotion, the fourth P of the marketing mix, which includes the communications process and the seven key decision areas of the promotional strategy.

Today's business world is highly competitive and changing fast, and marketing, as a body of knowledge and best practice, must respond to these changes. However, there is one fundamental fact about marketing that remains constant: it is that, to become successful and remain successful, an organization must be better at meeting customers' needs than the competition.

Eric Davies

SUNDAY

What is marketing?

Today we will set out to define marketing and to dispel some of the common misunderstandings regarding the meaning and nature of marketing. We will look at established UK and American definitions of marketing and some current European thinking about the definition of marketing for the 21st century. We will also summarize the history of marketing and how this business philosophy developed in response to increased competition.

We will consider the relationship between marketing and business performance and some of the key evidence to support the view that a 'customer/marketing orientation' can have a positive effect on profitability and performance.

We will also touch on the issue of competition and the need to consider the relationship between our customers/potential customers and our competitors in any discussion of our approach to marketing our business. We will return to this theme in more detail later in the week.

Finally today we will look at marketing and the business as a whole, and identify some of the key behaviours of businesses that have effectively (and profitably) made the customer/marketing orientation the basis of their operations.

Defining marketing

In essence, marketing is a relatively simple concept but at its root lies a fundamental approach to directing a business. Its simplicity can lead to the real meaning of marketing being misunderstood or misconstrued – and this can lull us into a false sense of security. And, if we don't understand what marketing is, we had better hope that our competitors don't know either – because, if they do, they will have a competitive advantage over us.

A good way to explain marketing is to start by dispelling two common misunderstandings regarding its meaning and nature.

- **Marketing is just a posh name for selling.** WRONG! A sale is often the ultimate objective of a marketing strategy, but marketing covers a much broader range of activities than just the sale event. Selling is the exchange of a product or service for, most commonly, a monetary value. Selling can be viewed as the last step in the marketing process. If marketing has been effective, it should make selling 'easier' (although selling is never easy!) because promotional and sales effort will have been directed at those customer groups who have a perceived need for the company's offering.
- **Marketing just means advertising.** WRONG! Promotion (including advertising) is a strategic activity that focuses on transmitting informative and/or persuasive messages via a medium or range of media to defined target audiences. In simple terms promotion is, again, *part* of the

marketing strategy (as we will see later). This potential misunderstanding is further compounded when news media talk about a 'marketing gimmick' when they mean a 'promotional gimmick'.

SUNDAY

MONDAY

TUESDAY

WEDNESDAY

THURSDAY

FRIDAY

SATURDAY

Some definitions of marketing

The UK Chartered Institute of Marketing (CIM) says that

'Marketing is the management process responsible for identifying, anticipating and satisfying consumers' requirements profitably.'

The American Marketing Association (AMA) defines marketing as

'the process of planning and executing the conception, pricing, promotion, and distribution of ideas, goods, and services to create exchanges that satisfy individual and organizational objectives.'

Both of these definitions are manifestations of the prevailing view of what constitutes marketing. However, a number of commentators are now suggesting that it is time to redefine marketing for the 21st century. For instance, one suggested definition, from C. Grönroos of the Swedish School of Economics, Helsinki, is:

'Marketing is to establish, develop and commercialize long-term customer relationships, so that the objectives of the parties involved are met. This is done by mutual exchange and keeping of promises.'

It is worth noting that both the AMA and Grönroos definitions refer to 'exchange'. At the heart of marketing is the process of enabling individuals and organizations to obtain what they need and want through exchanges with others.

For the purposes of this book a simple, usable definition might be:

'Marketing is the identification and anticipation of customers' needs and the profitable satisfaction of those needs.'

In essence, marketing is a business philosophy that says *it is easier to achieve your business objectives if you understand and meet customers' needs*. Customers should be the *raison d'être* of the business.

There are **four key issues** encompassed in our simple definition:

'Marketing is the identification and anticipation of customers' needs and the profitable satisfaction of those needs.'

1 **Identification** To be truly marketing oriented, a business must **identify** customer **needs**. Marketing research linked to marketing decision making is the hallmark of a marketing-oriented company.
2 **Satisfaction** Customers must feel that the **benefits** offered by the company's products or services **meet** their **needs**. If this does not happen, there is little opportunity for repeat sales.
3 **Profitable** Profit is an obvious business objective, and part of the 'consideration' (to use a term from contract law) for satisfying customer needs is to make a profit. In addition, for a business to survive and satisfy customer needs in the future, profit is essential.
4 **Anticipation** Part of what marketing needs to do is study customers' behaviour and attitudes to make it possible to **predict** how changes will affect future demand for products and services.

It is also important to stress that, when establishing and maintaining customer relationships, the seller gives a set of **promises** based on the performance of a product or service offered, i.e. the benefits inherent in the offering that the seller believes are matched to the needs of the customer. In return the buyer promises to meet his/her commitment in the exchange, generally some form of payment. Promise is a key component of marketing, not only during the first purchase but also as central to the ongoing relationship between buyers and sellers.

One way to get a better understanding is to take a brief look at the history of marketing.

A history of marketing

Some argue that marketing has been in existence whenever and wherever there have been buyers and sellers, i.e. a market. However, it is generally considered that marketing, as we understand it, developed when competition for customers intensified.

Before and during the Industrial Revolution (roughly 1750–1850 in the UK), goods were relatively scarce and producers could sell all that they could produce. The focus was therefore on production and distribution at the lowest cost. This approach to organizing a business is often referred to as a **'production orientation'**.

From the late 19th and early 20th centuries, competition grew and the focus turned to selling what could be produced, by persuading buyers to choose the seller's product, regardless of whether it was the best match to the customer's needs. A clear problem with this approach is that, if the product does not meet the customer's needs, they will not purchase it again. Consequently, there will be no repeat sales and this will impact on the survival of the business. This approach to organizing a business is often referred to as a **'sales orientation'**.

From the 1950s onwards, most markets displayed intense competition for customers, and this competition drove the need to understand and satisfy customers' needs if the business was to succeed. In essence, this approach puts the customer at the centre of a firm's thinking and strategy, an approach to organizing a business that we often refer to as a **'customer or marketing orientation'**.

Marketing was once seen as the preserve of fast-moving consumer goods (FMCG) companies; now marketing and its techniques can be found in most industries. Even the public sector and charities are embracing the marketing orientation. In not-for-profit environments the main differences are that the objectives of the organization may not be expressed in terms of profitability or market share, and there is generally no real 'competitive' element.

In addition, marketing became an important academic subject – there is a reference to 'marketing' in a course syllabus at Ohio State University from 1921 – and is a central plank of management education, both undergraduate and postgraduate, across the world. I recently 'Googled' the term 'marketing MBA' and got 87.8 million results!

It is important to point out that, even now, 'production-oriented' and 'sales-oriented' organizations can still be identified in some business sectors. This situation seems to be related to:

● the nature of the particular market environments of these sectors, e.g. large purchase values, very small number of customers, complex contractual arrangements
● the attitudes/perceptions of senior management in these sectors.

Perhaps such management has been sceptical about whether marketing helps improve business performance and has therefore been reluctant to adopt the customer/marketing orientation.

Marketing and business performance

Both managers and academics have long been exercised by the 'value' of marketing to a business. In other words, if your business is marketing orientated, will you be more profitable than businesses that are not?

From a manager's perspective, the issue is straightforward: why should you invest any scarce resource (including time and money) in marketing unless there is evidence that it will make you more profitable?

Academics have also focused on this issue, not only to support managers (by seeking to distil best practice) but also to understand the fundamental relationships between independent variables (such as what we do) and dependent variables (the results of what we do).

Academic research in this area began seriously in the 1970s. Probably one of the most important studies was the Profit Impact of Market Strategies (PIMS) study from Harvard University. The basis of the study was a huge survey and a large multiple regression model. It started with hundreds of independent variables that were considered to affect the key dependent variables (i.e. profit and return on investment (ROI), often referred to as return on capital employed (ROCE) in the UK) and finished up with 37 variables that explained most (80 per cent) of the causal effect. The study identified that profit margins and ROI are strongly, and positively, related to four key variables:

1 **business share of the target market**, relative to the share held by the top three competitors (relative market share)
2 **customer rating of product/service performance**, relative to competitors (customer perceived relative quality)
3 **asset productivity**, measured in terms of value added/capital employed
4 **employee productivity**, measured in terms of real value added per person.

As might be expected, a range of variables influences profitability, including those associated with the relationship between the business and its marketplace (including customers and competitors) and others within the firm (such as asset productivity and employee productivity, both related to the effective management of the business).

What seems to be clear from the PIMS study is that high market share is an important predictor of business performance. This is achieved by providing customers with the products/services that deliver benefits that they perceive match their needs best and this, fundamentally, is what marketing is all about. The second variable, customer perceived relative quality, confirms this: to be a leader in any market you must have a better offering than that of your competitors. So marketing, as a business philosophy and as a way of organizing a business, is one important independent variable affecting the key dependent variables of profit margin and ROI.

Researchers turned their attention to the relationship between 'customer/marketing orientation' (i.e. the implementation of the marketing concept encapsulated in our definition set out above) and business performance. During the 1990s, a number of key studies were published and most indicate a positive, if sometimes weak, relationship between customer/marketing orientation and business performance.

What we can say is that the evidence shows that a customer/
marketing orientation is associated with improved business
performance.

The four 'big ideas' in marketing

1 Exchange At the heart of marketing is the process of
enabling individuals and organizations to obtain what they
need and want through exchanges with others.

2 Promise In establishing and maintaining customer
relationships, the seller gives a set of promises based on
the performance of a product or service offered. In return
the buyer promises to meet his/her commitment in the
exchange, generally some form of payment.

3 Matching Marketing matches the benefits in the
organization's offerings with the customer's needs.

4 'Customer' or 'marketing' orientation A business that
is customer (or marketing) oriented puts customer needs
at the centre of their thinking and strategy.

Customers and the competition

One important aspect of the real-world situation we have
not addressed yet is competition. So far, the customer/
marketing orientation has placed the customer as the focus
of the business. This seems intuitively acceptable – if we
understand and meet customers' needs, we should win their

business – but while we are focusing on customers, so are our competitors. Consequently, any effective marketing strategy must take into account our competition and the relationship between them and our customers/potential customers.

The first issue to consider is the nature of the customers' perceived needs – the customer/marketing orientation. Customers will seek to identify the best match of benefits to their perceived needs and in doing so will make judgements about the various offerings available to them.

In addition, customers will consider the price of each competitor's offering along with the benefits they perceive in each offering. In essence, customers will make a value judgement – which offering provides the most benefits at the lowest price.

We will return to these issues in more detail later in the week.

Marketing and the business

A reasonable question to ask at this stage is this: if a customer/marketing orientation is linked to profitability, what is it we have to do to make it operational (and therefore effective) in our business?

A wide range of studies has distilled **five key behaviours** that characterize businesses which have effectively (and profitably) made customer/marketing orientation the operational basis of their businesses.

1 **Market sensing**

This is the foundation of an effective customer/marketing orientation. We must know what our customers' needs are and, to do this, we need to use a range of sources including direct contact with our customers and tools like marketing research (which we will look at later in the week). In addition, we know that we do not live in a static environment so therefore we need to track changes in customers' needs.

2 **Quality focus**

The PIMS research highlighted the relationship between product/service quality and business performance, and the message is that the business must seek to improve product/service quality to maintain a competitive differential. Clearly, this must include monitoring competitive actions.

3 Internal 'marketing'

It was once said that 'Marketing is too important to be left to the marketing department' and, like many humorous quotes, this has a strong basis in reality. While specialist marketing-related functions still exist, in many modern businesses large marketing departments have been replaced by a business-wide focus on satisfying customer needs. Quite simply, all employees must know what they have to do to satisfy customers' needs, must be able to do it and must be motivated to do it.

4 Adaptive response

We all know that we live in a time of rapid change and it is therefore critical that businesses are flexible and able to adapt to changing market conditions and customer needs. This includes understanding how broader political, economic, social and technological factors impact on our customers and competitors.

5 External relationships

It is all too easy for business managers to feel they must focus all their attention on matters within the business but, as we have seen, the success of the business depends on how we interact with the outside world. Constructing effective means of two-way communication with customers is therefore paramount. This can be as simple as ensuring that customers are encouraged to tell the business about problems or any gaps in meeting their needs to using sophisticated barcode/customer loyalty card data analysis and customer satisfaction research. Managers need to identify and focus on key account relationships (KAR), i.e. those accounts that are responsible for the majority of the business. Such KARs could be with your main customers or perhaps your major distributors/retailers.

Customer relationship management (CRM) programmes are designed to formalize the process of customer/ business relationships, with customer retention often a key objective. A number of software companies provide bespoke software to support the CRM function.

Summary

Developed as a strategic response to intensified competition for customers, marketing is a relatively simple concept but a fundamental approach to directing a business.

In essence, marketing is a business philosophy that says it is easier to achieve your business objectives if you understand and meet customers' needs, and research indicates that marketing improves business performance. Customers should be the *raison d'être* of the business.

Four 'big ideas' are central to marketing: exchange, promise, matching, and customer or marketing orientation. Another key aspect of strategic marketing is our competitors, who are also interacting with our customers/potential customers.

Finally, there are five key behaviours that characterize businesses which have effectively (and profitably) made customer/marketing orientation the operational basis of their businesses: market sensing, quality focus, internal marketing, adaptive response and external relationships.

SUNDAY
MONDAY
TUESDAY
WEDNESDAY
THURSDAY
FRIDAY
SATURDAY

Fact-check (answers at the back)

1. Why can the meaning of marketing be misunderstood?
   a) Because it is a relatively simple concept but a fundamental approach to directing a business ❏
   b) It is not related to the real world of business ❏
   c) It is a complex academic subject ❏
   d) It is only relevant to the US market ❏

2. How can marketing be defined?
   a) As a posh word for selling ❏
   b) It is the same as advertising and promotion ❏
   c) As the identification and anticipation of customers' needs and the profitable satisfaction of those needs ❏
   d) None of the above ❏

3. What is the business philosophy of marketing?
   a) Spending the most on advertising guarantees you a profit ❏
   b) It is easier to achieve your business objectives if you understand and meet customer needs ❏
   c) Customers will buy whatever you can produce ❏
   d) You only have to convince the customer once to be successful ❏

4. Persuading buyers to choose the seller's product regardless of whether it is the best match to the customer's needs is known as what?
   a) Production orientation ❏
   b) Sales orientation ❏
   c) Customer or marketing orientation ❏
   d) Retail orientation ❏

5. Why did companies start to embrace marketing from the 1950s onwards?
   a) There were more advertising media, such as TV, available ❏
   b) Advertising agencies had been invented ❏
   c) Most markets displayed intense competition for customers ❏
   d) Mail order was a new sales method ❏

6. What does the Profit Impact of Market Strategies (PIMS) study?
   a) The relationship between strategy and profit ❏
   b) The characteristics of the best managers ❏
   c) The size of the US export market ❏
   d) The differences between capitalist and communist systems ❏

7. What are the two marketing outcomes that PIMS identified as strongly and positively related to profitability?
a) Brand logo and colour ❏
b) Relative market share and customer perceived relative value ❏
c) Size and frequency of advertisements ❏
d) Range and content of sponsorship deals ❏

8. Why must a marketing strategy take the competition into account?
a) The rate of change in society is so fast ❏
b) They too are focusing on our customers/potential customers ❏
c) International trade is important ❏
d) The Internet is important ❏

9. What are market sensing, quality focus, internal 'marketing', adaptive response and external relationships?
a) Terms used in new product testing ❏
b) Sales management techniques ❏
c) Key behaviours of businesses that have effectively made customer/ marketing orientation an operational basis of their businesses ❏
d) None of the above ❏

10. What is a key concept of the customer/marketing orientation?
a) Exchange ❏
b) Promise ❏
c) Matching process ❏
d) All of the above ❏

MONDAY

Marketing and the customer

We learned yesterday that the customer is at the heart of the customer/marketing orientation and that it is easier to achieve our business objectives if we understand and meet customers' needs. Clearly, customers are very important to a business and to the development of marketing thought, and today we will focus on customers as individuals and as organizations.

We will begin by considering customers' motives, values and attitudes and how these influence the way they perceive their needs, and look at customer behaviour as a problem-solving process and the stages involved in that. We shall also review the differences between individual customers and organizational customers and look at the importance of decision-making units (DMUs) in the latter. We will review the importance of market segmentation and look at the ways in which markets can be segmented.

Finally, we will consider the impact of political, economic, social and technological (PEST) drivers that shape the world in which customers exist and therefore have a major influence on customers' behaviour.

Who are our customers?

A good place to start is with the question, 'Who are our customers?' At first sight this might seem a simple question. Our customers are the people who buy our products or services. Customers can be individuals, families, small and medium-sized businesses, public limited companies (PLCs), government departments, and so on. It is possible, therefore, to divide customers into two broad markets:

● **consumer markets** – e.g. individuals and families
● **organizational or business-to-business (B2B) markets** –
  e.g. businesses, not-for-profit/charitable organizations and
  government departments.

Customers in consumer markets

We can all relate to customers in consumer markets – a subject that is often referred to as consumer behaviour – since we are all customers: we all buy products and services as individuals.

Our definition of marketing focuses on 'customers' needs'. Some writers distinguish between a 'need' and a 'want': they say a need is something fundamental to life, such as water, food, shelter, etc., whereas a want is a desire to possess something that is less important to life. The *Concise Oxford English Dictionary* defines a 'need' as 'a want or requirement' and a 'want' as 'a desire, wish for possession, need'. For the purposes of understanding customers' needs, we can assume that a need and a want are one and the same.

When considering how customers perceive their needs, we have to embrace some concepts and knowledge developed in disciplines such as psychology and sociology. We are going to look at customers' motives, values and attitudes, and customer behaviour as a problem-solving process.

Motives

At the heart of a perceived need is a **driver**, a motive. Abraham Maslow produced a hierarchical structure of needs based on five core levels.

SUNDAY

MONDAY

TUESDAY

WEDNESDAY

THURSDAY

FRIDAY

SATURDAY

	Need	Motive
Lower level	Physiological	Water, sleep, food
	Safety	Security, shelter, protection
	Belongingness	Love, friendship, acceptance by others
	Ego	Prestige, status, accomplishment
Upper level	Self-actualization	Self-fulfilment, personal enrichment

At each level, different priorities exist in terms of the benefits a customer is seeking. The implication is that one must first satisfy basic needs before ascending to higher needs. Of course, one product or service may satisfy a number of different needs simultaneously. For example, a meal at a fashionable and expensive restaurant can meet a range of needs from physiological to ego and self-actualization.

Sex, in particular, transcends the levels of Maslow's hierarchy. A basic biological drive, sex is also a more complex motive that can involve belongingness, ego and self-actualization.

Many of the products and services we purchase in modern economic markets have a significant element of the upper-level motives at the root of our perceived needs. Examples include clothing (designer clothes and shoes) and cars (luxury saloon cars, performance cars, 'super cars').

Some commentators (e.g. J. K. Galbraith in his 1967 book *The New Industrial State*) have seen this as businesses exercising control over consumers through advertising and related salesmanship activities – in effect, creating artificial needs and wants among consumers.

Values

Our motives are filtered through our values. Values can be defined as our broad preferences concerning appropriate courses of action or outcomes and reflect our sense of 'good' and 'bad'. Our values develop in a number of ways but the family (socialization of children) is a major factor, along with school, religion and peer group influence.

For example, motives such as prestige and status (ego needs) would be manifested as different perceived needs in individuals with different values. We can take this example further if we consider the purchase of a prestige car: a customer whose values include a heightened sense of environmental issues is likely to have a different set of perceived needs from a customer who does not share that value. A hybrid vehicle would therefore not to be equally attractive to both customers.

Attitudes

Over time, we all develop a set of attitudes. Attitudes are a predisposition or a tendency to respond positively or negatively towards a certain stimulus – an idea, a person, a situation, a product, etc. Our attitudes incorporate both our motives and our values but are also influenced by our experiences.

For instance, following the tragedy at Hillsborough football stadium in Sheffield, England, in 1989, *The Sun* newspaper published an article accusing Liverpool fans of appalling behaviour on the day. There was no truth in these claims, and the people of Liverpool responded with justifiable anger. Sales of the newspaper on Merseyside plunged from 200,000 copies a day to just a couple of thousand. *The Sun*'s customers in Liverpool changed their attitude to the newspaper in a matter of days.

Behaviour

Customer behaviour has traditionally been seen as a problem-solving process. Implicit in this is that customers act in a logical manner when selecting solutions to their needs. The steps in the process are set out below.

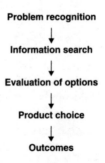

Problem recognition
↓
Information search
↓
Evaluation of options
↓
Product choice
↓
Outcomes

The problem-solving process

For some purchases (particularly more expensive ones) customers do actually follow such a process. However, for lower-cost (and therefore lower-risk) purchases evidence suggests that the decision process is significantly less rigorous. In addition, different customers go through more or less rigorous decision processes depending on their socio-economic and cultural situation.

Let's look at the different stages of the process in detail.

1 Problem recognition

Problem recognition is the point at which a customer articulates their 'perceived need' (see our definition of marketing from Sunday). In reality customers usually have a number of perceived needs that are important to them in meeting their overall needs. Such needs tend to have different levels of importance to them – the customer's 'hierarchy of needs' – a ranked list of those needs that must be satisfied to convince the customer to buy.

For major purchases (like a home or a car) customers may have a long list of perceived needs, sometimes running into double figures. Marketers have spent considerable effort to both identify and rank customers' needs in such situations. One important finding is that, even when there is a relatively long list of perceived needs, the actual purchase decision is often based on the three or four most important perceived needs.

2 Information search

The next stage can involve a wide range of activities, including looking at manufacturers' brochures and advertisements, reviews in magazines and reports from specialist consumer advisory groups (such as *Which?*) and making online searches for user blogs. Personal contacts, such as family, friends and colleagues, and word-of-mouth are also important sources of information and help with forming opinions.

3 Evaluation of options

To evaluate the options, the customer compares the benefits of a number of solutions (our offering and our competitors') against their perceived needs. The customer will decide which offering has the best match of benefits to their needs, and this will normally produce a ranking of best match to least good match. One element will be price.

The customer now has to decide which offering is the best **value**, i.e. represents the most benefits at the lowest price. This can be difficult for the customer when both the number of benefits and the price vary between offerings.

Second best?

During the 1970s a leading domestic durables manufacturer (we'll call them 'the client') commissioned a research study that asked customers to rank their product and competitive products in terms of the best match to the respondents' needs. In all the studies, the client's product topped the list. However, they achieved poor market share figures. Further research identified that the reason for this apparent contradiction (i.e. we have the best match of benefits to the customers' needs but they don't buy our product) was that the price differential between the client's product and the next best-ranked product was large enough to persuade customers to buy the second-ranked rather than the first-ranked offering.

4 Product choice

The penultimate stage in the problem-solving process, product choice, leads to the act of purchase. At this stage, buyers may experience pre-purchase anxiety, a worry about the ramifications of the act they are about to commit. Is it the right product for me? Can I afford it? Will my friends like it? In some cases this leads to the customer postponing a purchase decision. Marketers are obviously keen to minimize the effect of pre-purchase anxiety.

5 Outcomes

The final outcomes stage can be described as the 'consumption' stage, when the customer actually gets to consume the benefits carried by the offering. What we can see is that there are two stages when the customer is evaluating the product:

● the pre-purchase stage up to and including the purchase
● the post-purchase stage.

In the post-purchase stage the product must fulfil the promises made at the pre-purchase stage. Failure to do so will mean there is little likelihood of repeat purchase. This is an important business imperative: it is costly to 'create' a customer and, if we fail to satisfy them, we will provide an opportunity for our competitors.

Customers may also experience post-purchase anxiety – again experiencing the same worries that they may have had before the purchase. Marketers need to help customers deal with post-purchase anxiety by reinforcing the positive messages used at the pre-purchase stage. We will return to this on Saturday.

The customer decision is further complicated when the person who buys (i.e. pays for) the product or service is different from the person who consumes the product or service. For instance, when someone buys a present for another person, the buyer is not the consumer. In this situation the buyer is assessing whether the benefits they perceive in the offering will match the needs of the third party.

Other factors in decision making

Some of the current thinking about human decision making comes from the Nobel Prize winner Daniel Kahneman. In his book *Thinking, Fast and Slow* (2011) he presents evidence that humans are far from being 'rational agents' and are often inconsistent, emotional and biased in their decision making. Kahneman refers to two 'systems' of thinking. *System Two* is the conscious, thinking mind that considers, evaluates and reasons. *System One*, on the other hand, is responsible for the automatic and effortless mental response. *System One* works on as little or as much information as it has and is responsible for snap decisions regarding major courses of action including buying decisions. So *System One* thinking may lead a customer to select a product that they would reject if they adopted *System Two* thinking.

Neuromarketing is a further, parallel approach to looking at the brain from a marketing perspective. The term 'neuromarketing' is thought to have been coined by Ale Smidts of Erasmus University in the early 2000s and is the application of brain-scan technology, especially functional magnetic

resonance imaging (fMRI), to marketing problems. One of the findings indicates that brain activity for an action begins about half a second before a person consciously decides to take an action. This suggests that we are not so much consciously 'making' a decision as becoming aware that a decision has been made. These are early days for neuromarketing and we can expect more developments soon.

Customers in organizational or B2B markets

It is generally considered that organizational markets differ from consumer markets in four key ways.

1 B2B markets have a relatively small number of customers – e.g. there are relatively few car manufacturers in Europe.
2 Demand for products and services is 'derived demand', i.e. derived from the need to meet organizational objectives rather than to be consumed for their own sake, as is the case in consumer markets – e.g. car manufacturers buy steel sheet not for its own sake but as a part of the process of producing cars for consumption by consumers.
3 Decision making concerned with specifying and procuring products and services is normally a complex interaction of individuals within and sometimes from outside the organization (including consultants) – e.g. technical staff will specify and buying professionals will procure.

4 The perceived needs of the organization will involve a complex interaction of the stated corporate needs and the personal needs of the individuals involved in the decision. The company will specify what is required but this will be interpreted by individuals and will therefore be filtered through their own motives, values and attitudes.

Like consumer buyer behaviour, organizational buyer behaviour is a problem-solving process. However, in the latter case the stages of the process are normally more rigorous. There are eight steps.

Step 1 Need recognition

Step 2 Definition of the characteristics and quantity needed

Step 3 Development of the specifications to guide procurement

Step 4 Search for and qualification of potential sources

Step 5 Acquisition and analysis of proposals

Step 6 Evaluation of proposals and selection of supplier(s)

Step 7 Selection of an order routine

Step 8 Performance feedback and evaluation

It is worth comparing this with the model of individual customer behaviour as a problem-solving process, set out above. The similarities are quite clear and, again, the real difference is in the rigour required by organizations (which is not to say that some individuals do not also adopt very rigorous processes).

The eight steps set out above are associated with a **new-task** purchase situation in which an organization is buying a product or service for the first time. It involves greater potential risk and the involvement of the largest number of decision participants.

Some organizations use decision theory models to support the buying process. The steps in the process are as follows.

1 A list of selection criteria is assembled.

2 Each criterion is given a weight in terms of its importance.

3 Each identified potential supplier is scored on each criterion.

4 Suppliers are then ranked in terms of these weighted scores.

Once a selection has been made, purchases can become more routine, even automated, and this is known as **straight rebuy**.

Between the two extremes of new-task and straight rebuy is **modified rebuy**. In this case the organization needs to modify the specification, terms, price, etc., and this requires more decision participants than straight rebuy but not as many as new-task.

When the decision participants act together, they are known as a buying centre or a **decision-making unit (DMU)**. Research has identified five key roles in the DMU.

- **Users** Those who use the purchased item such as the production department
- **Influencers** Members of the organization who influence the purchasing decision even though they may not be centrally involved, e.g. members of the marketing department
- **Buyers** Those members of the organization who have authority to select suppliers and arrange terms of purchase
- **Deciders** Those members of the organization with formal or informal power to determine the final choice of supplier
- **Gatekeepers** Those individuals who control the flow of information into the organization and therefore indirectly influence the purchasing decision, e.g. members of the finance department through their control of budgets.

It has also shown that the DMU usually has one member (known as the 'salient member') who has the major influence on the selection decision. This person is not always the most senior member of the group, however. The DMU can contain a number of 'champions' who favour particular solutions.

Market segmentation

Customers are different – in their values and attitudes, their incomes, age, gender, location and so on – and these differences are the reason why marketing managers seek to **segment** markets. Segmentation refers to dividing customers into segments where customers within one segment have similar characteristics and as a segment are different from customers in other segments.

Examples of market segments

Geographical – countries, regions within countries, etc.

Demographic – based on age, gender, family size, income, occupation, education, race, religion, etc.

Behavioural – consumer knowledge, perceptions, attitudes, uses of and responses to a product or service.

Fundamentally, segmentation of a market must be based on differences in customers' perceived needs. However, in practical terms, it is sometimes difficult to identify (and therefore to direct marketing effort at) potential customers on this basis.

While it is relatively easy to identify customers/potential customers by age or gender or where they live, such variables do not always correspond to customers' buying preferences. This has led marketers to seek to record customers' preferences through mechanisms such as loyalty programmes (store cards, air miles). An alternative approach combines a range of data sources to profile customers and create segments based on customers' buying behaviour. For example, CACI Ltd ACORN is a geodemographic tool used to identify and understand the UK population and the demand for products and services.

Other characteristics of effective segmentation

Measurable We need to be able to measure the market – usually in terms of market worth (i.e. monetary spend) or number of customers. If we can't, it is difficult to develop strategies to exploit these segments.

Accessible We need to be able to access customers in terms of the media they are exposed to and where they shop. If we lack information about these factors, it is again difficult to develop strategies to exploit these segments.

Critical mass The segment must be big enough to make it cost-effective for the company to target it.

Recent research in *McKinsey Quarterly* (January 2011) suggests that businesses should consider more rather than fewer segments ('think in terms of 30–50 segments, not 5 or so').

> **'Defining and understanding these segments correctly is one of the most practical things a company can do to improve its strategy.'**
>
> 'Have you tested your strategy lately?' *McKinsey Quarterly*, January 2011

Effective segmentation is critical to successful strategic marketing and we shall return to this topic on Wednesday.

The 'PEST' environment

Finally, we need to remember that all customers are subject to the influences and pressures of the broader 'environment'. In this context we are using the term 'environment' to include the political, economic, social and technological (PEST) drivers that shape the world in which customers exist and that therefore have a major influence on customers' behaviour. We can expand each element.

- **Political** includes aspects such as law making and tax policy.
- **Economic** includes the general economic climate, rate of inflation and interest rates.
- **Social** includes the prevailing attitudes in society, e.g. attitudes to smoking, recycling and energy conservation.
- **Technological** includes the increasing use of mobile communications technology and alternative (non-fossil fuel) power sources.

Some analysts have added legal and rearranged the mnemonic to SLEPT; others have inserted environmental (the physical environment) factors and expanded it to PESTEL or PESTLE. The model has recently been further extended to STEEPLE and STEEPLED, adding ethics and demographic factors.

PEST factors have an influence not only on customers but also on all participants in the marketplace, including our organization, competitors, suppliers and distributors, and we shall return to this later.

Summary

Customers can be individuals or organizations. Behind every perceived consumer need is a driver or *motive*. Motives are filtered through our *values*, our broad preferences concerning appropriate and good actions or outcomes. Family, school, religion and peer group are major influences on these.

The *attitudes* we develop are our tendency to respond positively or negatively towards certain stimuli. Our attitudes incorporate our motives and values but are also affected by our experiences. Customer behaviour has traditionally been seen as a *problem-solving process*. PEST drivers in the wider environment influence this behaviour.

Organizational markets differ from consumer markets in four key ways: they are smaller, demand is derived from organizational objectives, decisions are made by groups of participants, and perceived needs contain corporate and personal elements.

Effective *market segmentation* divides customers into measurable and accessible segments of appropriate critical mass according to differences in perceived needs.

Fact-check (answers at the back)

1. What is at the heart of a perceived need?
   a) An advertisement ❑
   b) A motive ❑
   c) A film ❑
   d) A book ❑

2. What, according to Maslow, is the lowest level need?
   a) Physiological level ❑
   b) Wants level ❑
   c) Ego level ❑
   d) Self-actualization level ❑

3. What does Maslow consider motives such as self-fulfilment and personal enrichment to be?
   a) Spending to the limit on your credit cards ❑
   b) Self-actualization needs ❑
   c) Basic needs ❑
   d) Being wealthy ❑

4. What are values?
   a) Our broad preferences concerning appropriate courses of action or outcomes ❑
   b) Our ability to detect falsehoods ❑
   c) Our ability to solve puzzles ❑
   d) Our ability to recall dreams ❑

5. What are attitudes?
   a) Our ability to play sports ❑
   b) Our ability to learn a musical instrument ❑
   c) Our ability to tell jokes ❑
   d) A predisposition to respond positively or negatively towards a certain stimulus ❑

6. What has customer behaviour traditionally been seen as?
   a) A problem-solving process ❑
   b) Linked to advertising ❑
   c) Totally linked to the weather ❑
   d) Unexplainable ❑

7. Why are organizational markets different from consumer markets?
   a) There are relatively few customers in organizational markets ❑
   b) Demand is derived from the needs of the organization ❑
   c) Decision making is complex and involves both organizational needs and the personal needs of the individuals involved ❑
   d) All of the above ❑

8. In the decision-making unit (DMU), what does the 'gatekeeper' role involve?
   a) Making sure the doors are closed ❑
   b) Controlling the flow of information ❑
   c) Preventing non-DMU members from entering the room ❑
   d) Keeping the minutes to the meeting ❑

9. In addition to differences in customers' perceived needs, for market segmentation to be effective what do the segments need to be?

a) Measurable ❏
b) Accessible ❏
c) An appropriate critical mass ❏
d) All of the above ❏

10. What are the elements of the PEST 'environment'?

a) Painting, English, sociology and training ❏
b) Power, engineering, selling and transport ❏
c) Processes, experiences, solutions and testing ❏
d) Political, economic, social and technological ❏

TUESDAY

Marketing information and marketing research

Marketers need information to reduce risk in decision making and to improve the effectiveness of the way they allocate scarce resources.

We will consider the American Marketing Association's (AMA) definition of MR and look at the elements of this definition and at some examples of research applications.

Today we will cover:

- research within the organization – types of information generated by the organization and the more formal marketing information system (MkIS) used by some companies
- marketing intelligence – its nature and some examples of sources of marketing intelligence
- secondary research – its nature and some examples of the four main sources of secondary research
- primary research – we will set out a model for the primary research process and look in some detail at each element including sampling frame and sampling, research instruments (particularly the questionnaire), question content and type, data collection methods, analysis and reporting.

What is marketing research?

On Sunday we said that marketing research (MR), linked to marketing decision making, is the hallmark of a marketing-oriented company. Identifying customers' needs is an essential element of marketing and, as we then saw on Monday, understanding customers' motives and buying behaviour is complex and MR is central to how we do this.

> ## A definition of marketing research
>
> The American Marketing Association (AMA) defines MR as follows.
>
> *Marketing research is the function that links the consumer, customer, and public to the marketer through information – information used to identify and define marketing opportunities and problems; generate, refine, and evaluate marketing actions; monitor marketing performance; and improve understanding of marketing as a process. Marketing research specifies the information required to address these issues, designs the method for collecting information, manages and implements the data collection process, analyses the results, and communicates the findings and their implications.*

There are three key issues encompassed in the comprehensive definition shown in the box above.

1 **MR acts as a link** between the customer and the organization and allows a two-way flow of information; the organization can use research to understand the customer and can present the customer with ideas and offerings and gauge the customers' likes and dislikes.

2 **MR captures information** about marketing opportunities and problems; the purpose of research therefore is to reduce risk in decision making and help managers make better and more successful decisions.

3 **MR is a process** involving research design, data collection, analysis and communication of the findings.

Marketing research is an investment for organizations: they are investing resources (normally money) to reduce the risk of wrongly allocating a scarce resource or failing to maximize an opportunity. Consequently, there is a trade-off between the cost of MR and the benefit the organization will obtain in reducing risk in decision making. Clearly, the higher the perceived risk, the more managers are likely to be prepared to invest in MR.

To understand the scope of MR, consider some examples of applications:

- market/segment size and trends – focusing on establishing the size (monetary value, unit value) of a market and/or segments of the market
- customer need analysis and attitudes to competitive offerings – to establish the perceived needs that a customer group (or segment) holds regarding a defined product/service, the ranking of these needs in their minds, and their perceptions of the benefits inherent in the various offerings (the client's and their competitors') available to them
- customer care research – to monitor customers' levels of satisfaction, etc.
- corporate identity research – to support the development or updating of a company's corporate identity
- message research – to test the effectiveness of different promotional messages
- new product development (NPD) research – assessing the appeal of a new product to a market segment.

This chapter will look at research within the organization, marketing intelligence, secondary research and primary research.

Research within the organization

It is important to place MR within the overall organizational information process. Modern information technology (IT) enables organizations to produce a wide range of information including financial and accounting, production and process. From a marketing perspective, businesses also generate a wide range of information concerning the relationship between the organization and its customers. For instance:

- sales volumes – by product range, etc.
- sales trends – tracked over time, seasonality, etc.
- sales by segment – type of customer, geographical location, etc.
- requests for product information – responses to 'advertisements, website 'hits', etc.
- complaints – obviously it is important that complaints are dealt with effectively, but complaints also provide a useful source of information: customers who complain may be articulating the view of a larger, silent group of customers
- reports from salespeople – particularly in B2B markets, sales reports are very important in managing the marketing/sales effort.

Many organizations have an established formal process known as a **marketing information system (MkIS)**.

A definition of a marketing information system

An MkIS is a system in which marketing data are formally gathered, stored, analysed and distributed to managers in accordance with their informational needs on a regular basis.

The MkIS process involves four stages.

1 **Information requirements** An MkIS starts with a definition of the information requirements, i.e. the information required by managers to help them reduce risk in decision making.
2 **Data sources** The MkIS will draw on a wide range of information both from within the business (as suggested above) and from other sources outside the business. External sources include:

- marketing intelligence
- secondary research
- primary research (qualitative and quantitative).

3 **Data processing (to generate information)** There is a difference between data and information. Data are the raw facts, which may not necessarily be related to helping management reduce risk in decision making. Modern IT systems can generate significant volumes of data that can threaten to engulf managers. Information, on the other hand, is knowledge relevant to a specific requirement. The critical focus for the MkIS is that it must produce information appropriate to the decision needs of the users.

4 **Dissemination of information** For the information to be of value it must be disseminated to those who can obtain value from it. It is therefore important that the output of the MkIS is designed to meet the needs of the users, i.e. it is relevant, easily understood, clear and concise.

Marketing intelligence

There is a fairly strong link between marketing intelligence and secondary research. Marketing intelligence sources include customers, intermediaries, competitors, suppliers, new employees and the PEST environment.

> ## A definition of marketing intelligence
>
> *Marketing intelligence is the process of gathering and analysing information relevant to reducing risk in decision making from sources that are not formal marketing research sources.*

Customers

Particularly in B2B markets, companies can learn a great deal from maintaining a close dialogue with their customers, in addition to formal client relationship management (CRM) or marketing research studies.

Intermediaries

Many businesses use intermediaries such as retailers, wholesalers and distributors to take their products to market. Intermediaries are closer to the customer and often purchase from our competitors as well as from us. Intermediaries offer an excellent marketing intelligence source.

Competitors

Competitors are an excellent source of marketing intelligence. Their annual reports provide performance information, commentary on their strategy (Chairman's and CEO's statements) and information about future initiatives. Reports for all UK limited companies are available from Companies House www.companieshouse.gov.uk.

Also, competitors place information in the public domain to inform and persuade customers and potential customers: on their websites, in press releases (published in the business and general press), in publicity material, at exhibitions and on social networking sites, for instance. Some companies take studying their competitors to quite exhaustive lengths including monitoring their recruitment advertising to see what type and number of employees they are seeking to hire.

Suppliers

In a similar way to intermediaries, suppliers offer a good source of marketing intelligence. They are 'upstream' from our customers but are also likely to be focusing on our customers as part of their strategic activity. In addition, they are likely to supply our competitors as well as us and so have an understanding of our competitors' strategies.

New employees

Industries and sectors can be quite 'incestuous'. Companies are often trying to attract the same type of employee, and experienced new employees are likely to have worked with one or more of our competitors. Some businesses have formal 'debriefing' sessions for new employees to obtain information from them regarding customers and competitors.

PEST

We have seen that the broader 'environment' has a marked effect on our customers and, as we will see later, on both our business and our competitors. Consequently, it is important that our marketing intelligence monitors trends and changes in our PEST environment. Businesses engage with specialist associations and trade bodies, and maintain strong links with appropriate public bodies, to help them obtain 'early warning' of opportunities or threats that may be approaching.

Secondary research

Secondary research can be described as research conducted by others, not necessarily focusing on our particular information needs. It offers the advantages of relatively low cost (compared with primary research) and is often instantly available. Moreover, some research, such as a national census, would be impossible for one organization to undertake.

However, there are drawbacks. Because secondary research does not necessarily focus on our particular information needs, care must be taken not to 'fit' the needs of the research to the information available. Also, as the research is already available, it may be too old to meet the researcher's requirements. Fundamentally, the researcher must assess the degree of accuracy of the secondary research in terms of both how and when it was gathered, analysed and interpreted.

A huge range of information can be accessed through Internet search engines but, when assessing any particular source, take care to consider both the advantages and drawbacks set out above.

There are four main sources of secondary research: government, non-departmental public bodies, trade and professional bodies, and commercial research.

Government

Governments are the main source of secondary research. They conduct research as part of the process of government and the scope of the research therefore covers virtually all aspects of life. By way of illustration, we can look at three sources.

- **UK Office for National Statistics (ONS)** (www.ons.gov. uk) collects data and conducts research on a wide range of themes including the economy, business and energy, agriculture and environment, education, health and social care, the labour market and population (including the census data). Most reports are available as free downloads and some data are available as data sets that the user can construct into tables to meet their particular needs.
- **European Commission Eurostat** (www.epp.eurostat.ec.europa. eu) provides a very similar service for the 27 European Union (EU) countries as ONS does for the UK. Over a number of years the EU has harmonized the data collection activities of member states to allow for like-for-like comparisons.
- **US Dept of Commerce, Bureau of Economic Analysis** (www. bea.gov) follows a similar format both in terms of content and flexibility to ONS and Eurostat.

Non-departmental public bodies

Non-departmental public bodies (NDPBs) are set up to provide regulation to specific sectors. Examples in the UK include Ofwat (the Water Services Regulation Authority) and Ofcom (the independent regulator and competition authority for the communications industries). More general agencies include the following:

- **the Competition Commission** (www.competition-commission. org.uk) publishes reports on investigations into particular businesses in the UK

- **the Office of Fair Trading** (www.oft.gov.uk) publishes reports on investigations into particular UK industries.

Trade and professional bodies

These organizations representing particular industries or professions collect data and conduct research to inform their members and to provide evidence for public relations and lobbying. For example:

- **the Society of Motor Manufacturers and Traders** (www.smmt.co.uk) publishes a wide range of reports, e.g. *Motor Industry Facts*, a profile of the UK motor industry
- **the Law Society** (www.lawsociety.org.uk) represents solicitors in the UK and their research department publishes reports such as *Trends in the solicitors' profession*, an annual statistical report that presents a profile of the profession.

Commercial research

A number of organizations sell research studies they have already conducted (known as multi-client research). Some organizations cover a wide range of products and services while others specialize in specific sectors. Here are three good examples.

- **Mintel** (www.mintel.com) focuses particularly on consumer markets, e.g. mobile phones and network providers in the UK.
- **Keynote** (www.keynote.co.uk) has a mainly UK focus and includes non-consumer markets, e.g. arts and media sponsorship.
- **Euromonitor** (www.euromonitor.com) carries out international research covering a wide range of products and services, e.g. Apparel in the USA.

Primary research

Primary research refers to research designed and conducted to meet specific research needs. Often it builds on secondary research, but primary research will engage directly with the defined marketplace.

1 **Quantitative**

This uses some form of random sampling and structured data collection (such as a questionnaire). The findings from quantitative research are representative of the population from which the sample is drawn within defined levels of representativeness, and they can be presented in quantitative form, e.g. '65 per cent of respondents think our product is very good.' Many people will be familiar with quantitative research from being asked to participate in a survey or from seeing survey findings (such as opinion poll results) referred to in the media.

2 **Qualitative**

Qualitative research focuses more on understanding the underlying motives and drivers for people's actions. Typically, judgement rather than random sampling is used, and sample sizes are much smaller. Consequently, the findings cannot be said to be representative in quantitative terms (as in quantitative research). Qualitative research uses tools such as depth interviews and focus groups.

3 **Observation**

This involves gathering data by observing relevant people, actions and situations and is selected when researchers cannot obtain the required information through direct questioning. Observation can include using trained observers (e.g. observing customers' behaviour in a supermarket) and machine-based observation (e.g. electronic counting of foot fall into a shopping mall).

4 **Experimental**

Control samples (two samples drawn from different populations, for instance) are used to obtain causal information about links between independent variables (e.g. socio-economic group, age, gender) and dependent variables (e.g. product preferences).

The primary research process

Primary research is a process that can be illustrated as follows.

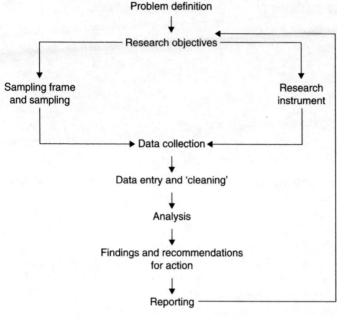

The primary research process

We can look at each part of the process in turn.

Problem definition

It is essential that the problem is clearly defined. One major issue is that the actual problem can be confused with the symptoms of the problem, and this confusion can lead to misdirected research effort. There is an old adage in consulting that says, 'A problem well defined is half solved.'

Research objectives

This stage establishes the foundation of the research study; all other stages will be based on the research objectives. Some researchers draw up a 'need-to-know' (N2K) list with the research user to ensure that all information requirements are covered by the study.

Sampling frame and sampling

The sampling frame is the 'population' of units under study, also known as the 'target population'. Units can be any group that the researcher is focusing on (e.g. individuals, households, businesses). Sampling refers to taking a representative portion of the target population. Clearly, a census (i.e. taking all units in the target population) provides the highest level of representativeness, but in most cases the cost and the time required to execute the research are prohibitive. There are two broad approaches to sampling.

- **Probability (or random) sampling** Simple random sampling means that each unit in the target population has the same chance (probability) of being sampled. There are other forms of probability sampling and one used quite extensively is stratified random sampling. In this the sample is drawn in line with the profile of the target population under study; so if 60 per cent of a target population is over the age of 50, then the sample would reflect this by ensuring that 60 per cent of the sample was also over that age.
- **Non-probability sampling** As the name suggests, this form of sampling is not based on units having the same chance (probability) of being sampled. Non-probability sampling can be selected for a number of reasons: for instance, a B2B company may wish to discover the attitudes and perceptions of their major customers and would therefore want specific individuals to be included in the target population. Qualitative research often uses a form of non-probability sampling.

There are two other aspects of sampling we need to consider.

- **Representativeness** Researchers and users of research need to know how representative a sample is of the target population from which it is drawn. There are two elements, allowable error and level of confidence. **Allowable error** is defined as the difference between the value achieved from the sample and the true value for the population. This is normally expressed as a ±%. **Level of confidence** is defined as the probability that the true value (for the population) will fall within the interval created by adding and subtracting the allowable error.

- **Sample size** is a function of the degree of variability in the population under study and the level of accuracy of representativeness required. If all the units in a population are identical, we will need to sample only one unit, regardless of the size of the population. Where researchers do not know the degree of variability in the population (which is often the case), they take the worst-case scenario and assume that the population is equally split on any measure.

The following table shows the relationship between three examples of sample size and the associated degrees of allowable error and levels of confidence.

Sample size	Level of confidence 95%	Level of confidence 90%
500	±4.4%	±3.7%
1,000	±3.1%	±2.6%
1,500	±2.5%	±2.1%

Allowable error (±) at 95 and 90 per cent levels of confidence associated with various sample sizes

You will note that as the sample size increases, so the allowable error decreases. The higher the level of confidence, the greater the allowable error is for the same sample size.

Research instrument

The research instrument is the means by which primary data are gathered. Some research designs use electronic or mechanical devices to gather data. Examples include website counts of 'hits', meters attached to viewers' televisions to monitor the programmes they watch, and eye cameras to study viewers' eye movements when watching advertisements. The main method of gathering primary data, however, is the **questionnaire**.

Questionnaires are a systematic way of gathering data and can broadly be divided into structured and semi-structured. A structured questionnaire is one where questions and potential answers are set up in advance (often using 'closed' questions); a semi-structured questionnaire uses a list of topics and allows the respondent to answer in their own words. Generally, structured questionnaires are used in quantitative research and semi-structured questionnaires are used in qualitative research, although there are times when formats are mixed.

Question content It is important that questions are drafted in a way that ensures that the respondents' views are recorded as accurately as possible. Questions (or statements) should aim to avoid:

- leading the respondent – e.g. 'Shopping centres are better than high streets.'
- embarrassing or pressurizing the respondent – e.g. questions about income/wealth or sexuality must be worded sensitively to ensure accurate and complete responses
- creating a status bias – e.g. 'Most intelligent shoppers compare prices. Do you?'
- ambiguous questions – questions must be unambiguous to prevent respondents interpreting the words differently, which would introduce a bias to the study.

Question types As mentioned above, there are two broad question types.

- **Open questions** allow the respondent to answer in his/her own words. This type captures the respondents' actual words but open questions are much more difficult to analyse than closed questions.
- **Closed questions** are those where the answers are set up in advance and are therefore much easier to analyse. However, closed questions 'force' the respondent to choose an answer and care must be taken to ensure that his/her opinion is represented in the predetermined list. One approach to dealing with this problem is to include an 'open' element in a closed question, e.g. 'Other, please state'.

The following are some of the most commonly used closed question types.

- **Dichotomous questions** require a simple Yes/No answer, e.g. 'Is this your first visit?'
- **Multiple-choice questions** offer the respondent several options: the respondent may be instructed to select only one option or, alternatively, all that are appropriate to them.

- **Projective questions** use a more indirect approach and techniques like sentence completion, word association, pictorial (e.g. adding words to a picture) and storytelling.
- **Attitudinal scales** Measuring attitudes is important and researchers use a range of scales. Some of the most widely used scales are:
  - itemized – various responses are itemized to help the respondent make his/her selection, as follows:

Buy every day	Buy once a week	Buy monthly	Buy rarely	Don't buy at all
1	2	3	4	5

  - constant sum – the respondent is asked to divide up or allocate a number of points (normally 100) to indicate the relative importance of two or more attributes, e.g. 'Please divide up 100 points to reflect how important any of the following features are to you.'
  - Likert – this scale is a symmetrical agree–disagree scale where each point in the scale has a constant value relationship with the other points. In some cases the middle point is removed to create a 'forced' response, i.e. the respondent has to agree or disagree. Likert scales are complex to develop and most researchers use currently tested versions.

Strongly agree	Agree	Neither agree nor disagree	Disagree	Strongly disagree
+2	+1	0	-1	-2

  - semantic differential – this scale uses bipolar adjectives (hot–cold, reliable–unreliable, old–new, etc.) and is often constructed with seven categories between the two poles allowing the respondent to select the position that best matches their opinion.

Hot						Cold
*	*	*	*	*	*	*

Data collection

Data collection is a form of communication: the researcher poses a question and the respondent answers. There are four broad data collection approaches, two of which involve an interviewer and two of which are based on self-completion.

- **Face-to-face (f2f) interviewing** includes the 'street intercept' interviews that many of us have experienced while shopping. This is the most versatile and productive method but it is also the most expensive. The method allows for in-home interviewing, which is particularly valuable when sampling is based on the demographic distribution of a population. Trained interviewers conduct the interview, often using CAPI (computer-assisted personal interviewing) systems to aid the process.

... AS SOMEONE WHO FITS OUR TYPICAL CUSTOMER PROFILE, ...

- **Telephone interviewing** again uses a trained interviewer and can also involve computer-based systems to aid the process (CATI or computer-aided telephone interviewing). This method is the fastest and is not as expensive as f2f but it lacks the more personal contact between the interviewer and respondent provided by f2f and is therefore not so versatile.
- **Self-completion postal questionnaires** are posted to respondents who are asked to complete the questionnaire and return it in a pre-paid envelope. This is a less expensive

method than both f2f and telephone. However, non-response rates are much higher with postal surveys and a major issue is the problem of non-response error – i.e. if those who do respond are different from those who do not, this may skew the results. In practice, researchers use a range of techniques to maximize response rates (e.g. primer letters, reminder letters, incentives) and also test for the likely direction of non-response error.

● **Self-completion web surveys** are a new method made available to researchers by the rapid growth of the Internet. Also based on self-completion, they are less expensive. Web-based surveys can use questionnaires on a website or send them out by email. The Internet can be valuable for researching groups that are difficult to reach through other methods (e.g. heavy web users such as teenagers). The main drawback is again the problem of non-response error.

Focus groups

Focus groups are a standard qualitative data collection technique used to capture respondents' views and attitudes about a subject. A focus group is generally made up of a group of respondents drawn from a defined 'population'. The group meets under the guidance of a 'moderator' who introduces topics to the group for discussion.

Data entry and 'cleaning'

Data collected are generally entered into an electronic database, either directly in the case of computer-aided data collection (such as CATI and CAPI) or manually where completed questionnaires are returned as 'hard copy'. In the latter case the process of transferring the data from the questionnaire to the database can be a source of error and it is therefore important to control for such error. The researcher must be sure that what is contained in the questionnaire is identical to that entered to the database for analysis. Researchers take a random sample of entered questionnaires and compare them with the original completed questionnaires to ensure accuracy.

An alternative to manual data entry is questionnaire scanning involving a scanner and dedicated software. In addition, the researcher will be concerned that the questionnaire has been completed correctly. For instance, a particular response to a question may ask the respondent to go to another section of the questionnaire (known as 'gate' questions). Sometimes, particularly in self-completion, a respondent may complete the wrong section and this type of error needs to be 'cleaned' before analysis.

Analysis

Analysis of data has been supported by specialist software since the 1970s and became available on PCs in the 1980s. Today there is a wide range of providers of data analysis software available, e.g. SPSS and SNAP.

Primary research data in a database has two elements: the **cases** (the respondents) and the **variables** (the information captured by the questions). A question in a questionnaire can have more than one variable, such as in the case of multiple-choice questions.

The starting point in analysing the data is to run a simple count of the numbers of responses in each category for each variable, known as **frequency analysis** or one-way tabulation. Here's an example.

1 Value label	2 Value	3 Frequency	4 Percentage	5 Valid percentage	6 Cumulative percentage
Yes	1	90	32.14	32.14	32.14
No	2	180	64.29	64.29	96.43
Don't know	3	10	3.57	3.57	100.0
Total		**280**	**100.0**	**100.0**	

1 The value labels: the predetermined answers to the question. In this example the question would have been a dichotomous question (Yes/No answer) with a Don't know option.

2 The 'value' or coding (1 = Yes, etc.) assigned to the value label and entered in the database.

3 The number of respondents by each category (Yes, No, Don't know) for this variable = the frequency of that answer. The total sample size in this example was 280.

4 The simple percentage values for each value label: here the majority of respondents (64 per cent) had answered No to this question.

5 If some respondents do not answer all the questions the software recalculates the percentage value based on the actual total number of respondents to that question. Here all respondents have responded, so the values in columns 5 and 4 are the same.

6 The cumulative percentage count based on column 4.

The next most common level of analysis counts two variables simultaneously. This is known as **cross-tabulation**. Cross-tabulation allows a researcher to investigate relationships between dependent variables (such as respondents' attitudes and behaviour) and independent variables (such as their age, gender, socio-economic position). As we saw on Monday, these relationships are important to the marketer. Below is an example of a cross-tabulation of gender and agreement/disagreement with a cited statement.

Value label	Value		Strongly agree	Agree	Disagree	Strongly disagree	Total
Male	1	Frequency	6	25	45	21	**97**
		Percentage	6.2	25.8	46.4	21.6	**100.0**
Female	2	Frequency	18	36	76	23	**153**
		Percentage	11.8	23.5	49.7	15.0	**100.0**
Total		**Frequency**	**24**	**61**	**121**	**44**	**250**
		Percentage	**9.6**	**24.4**	**48.4**	**17.6**	**100.0**

This cross-tabulation shows that there is little difference in agreement/disagreement with the cited statement between male and female respondents.

To further the researcher's understanding of the data, a wide range of statistical tests can be used.

Findings and recommendations for action

We have seen that the primary research process is a complex project management of a number of interrelated elements. This stage of the process must bring meaning and value to the research user. The starting point is to link the findings to the research objectives, assembling them in line with each element of the objectives.

Reporting

The way the findings are presented to users must be appropriate to their needs. Often this means using:

- **graphical representations** – e,g, pie charts, histograms
- **data 'reduction'** – i.e. simplifying numbers such as rounding them to make them easier to digest, e.g. 45.67 per cent 'reduced' to 46 per cent
- **summaries** – using 'executive' summaries, abstracts, etc.
- **presentations** – e.g. PowerPoint presentations.

Omnibus surveys and agencies

Omnibus surveys are multi-client surveys, so called because clients can join and leave the 'omnibus' according to their needs. The advantages to the research client include cost savings (because the sampling and screening costs are shared across multiple clients) and timeliness (because omnibus samples are large and interviewing is ongoing). For further information go to www.ipsos-mori.com/omnibusservices.aspx

While it is feasible for organizations to conduct their own research studies, managers often choose to use **marketing research agencies** because of their experience and expertise. In addition, agencies bring emotional detachment to the problem and by providing extra resources enable client staff to concentrate on their core objectives. For more information about selecting and commissioning MR agencies, visit www.mrs.org.uk

Summary

Marketing research (MR) acts as a link between customer and organization. It is an investment for organizations, and there is a trade-off between the cost and the benefit obtained in capturing information that reduces risk in decision making.

MR can be applied to many marketing problems including establishing segment size, and defining customers' needs or attitudes to the benefits perceived in different products. Modern IT enables organizations to produce information valuable for marketing decision making.

Secondary research is research that has been conducted by others, not necessarily focusing on our needs. The major sources are government, public bodies, trade/professional bodies and commercial research providers.

The primary research process involves defining the problem, research objectives, sampling frame and method, and research instrument and questions. When the data have been collected using an appropriate method, the findings are analysed and can be reported.

SUNDAY
MONDAY
TUESDAY
WEDNESDAY
THURSDAY
FRIDAY
SATURDAY

Fact-check (answers at the back)

1. What is a key issue of the AMA definition of marketing research (MR)?
   a) It's a link between customer and organization ❏
   b) It's another name for the R&D department ❏
   c) It's specific to pharmaceutical businesses ❏
   d) It's mainly an American activity ❏

2. What is a system that formally gathers, analyses and distributes information to managers known as?
   a) A talking shop ❏
   b) A marketing information system ❏
   c) An in-house website ❏
   d) A company newsletter ❏

3. What is information gathered about the general marketing environment including customers, intermediaries, competitors, suppliers and the general PEST environment known as?
   a) Office gossip ❏
   b) Marketing intelligence ❏
   c) Making contacts ❏
   d) Networking ❏

4. What is secondary research?
   a) Research conducted by others, not necessarily focusing on our particular needs ❏
   b) Research conducted after the main research ❏
   c) Research that is of less value ❏
   d) Research conducted by our customers ❏

5. Why is quantitative research different from qualitative research?
   a) There is much more of it ❏
   b) The results from quantitative research can be presented in quantitative form, e.g. 65% like our product ❏
   c) It can only be done by academics ❏
   d) It is free ❏

6. What is sampling, where each unit has the same chance of being sampled, known as?
   a) Probability or random sampling ❏
   b) Unknown sampling ❏
   c) Researcher's sampling ❏
   d) Explainable sampling ❏

7. What are the two broad question types?
- a) Right and wrong ☐
- b) Open and closed ☐
- c) Short and long ☐
- d) Difficult and easy ☐

8. What is one of the problems with self-completion data collection (including web-based)?
- a) Analysing them ☐
- b) Non-response bias ☐
- c) Preventing fraud ☐
- d) Handling complaints ☐

9. A primary research database has which two elements?
- a) Time and cost ☐
- b) Completed and aborted ☐
- c) Right and wrong ☐
- d) Cases and variables ☐

10. What is cross-tabulation?
- a) An error report ☐
- b) Corrupted data ☐
- c) Analysis of two variables simultaneously ☐
- d) Processing of incorrect cases only ☐

WEDNESDAY

Strategic marketing

Today we shall consider marketing as a strategic activity – how marketers decide what they must do to meet the organization's objectives. Marketing strategy can be seen as a marketing decision process involving a series of steps to analyse, plan, implement and control a range of activities designed to achieve the organization's objectives.

We will start by considering how marketers must review the strengths and weaknesses of their own organization (business audit) and assess the opportunities and threats in the marketplace (market audit) before conducting a 'targeting' exercise that matches the strengths of the organization to opportunities presented by different market segments. We will then see how marketers develop an integrated marketing strategy (marketing mix), and implement and control the execution of the strategy to meet the organization's objectives.

Finally today we will look at three famous approaches to developing strategy: the Boston Box, the Ansoff Box and Porter's Three Generic Strategies.

Marketing planning

Marketing planning is a strategic activity; marketers have to make a range of decisions that translate into actions in the future to achieve their objectives. Marketers have to **plan** and they have to develop a **strategy**.

> ## Two definitions
>
> **Plan** – a formulated and especially detailed method by which a thing is to be done; a design or scheme
>
> **Strategy** in game theory, business theory, etc. – a plan for successful action based on the rationality and interdependence of the moves of opposing or competing participants

Planning in marketing seeks to apply a logical and objective approach to deciding how a company's capabilities will be matched to opportunities in the marketplace so that the corporate objectives can be met. Strategy takes into consideration the 'moves' of others. For marketers, the key group of 'others' is competitors, i.e. 'opposing or competing participants'. However, for marketers, a key additional participant group is customers, whom we are neither 'opposing' nor 'competing' with. On first sight, these militaristic terms may seem to contradict the basic ethos of the marketing orientation we described on Sunday. The reason they are used in this context is that they reflect the nature of the process of deploying the organization's resources to achieve a defined objective.

Developing a strategic marketing plan involves a series of interrelated stages of analysis, planning, implementation and control. One might say that there are two broad elements to strategic marketing planning – thinking and doing. The ancient Greek proverb 'Think slowly, act quickly' extols the virtue of taking time to weigh up the options before acting, but it stresses the need to carry out the selected strategy without delay. Thinking helps us to reduce the risk in deciding what we should do and therefore significantly improves the probability

of success. This simple proverb encapsulates the value of
strategic marketing planning for the marketer.

The marketing planning process

We can translate the four stages of strategic marketing
planning into a marketing planning process, as shown below.

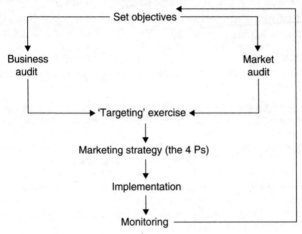

The marketing planning process

We shall consider each part of the process in turn.

Objectives

The organization will need to establish a set of objectives for
the planning period (probably 12 months). It is likely that setting
objectives will start with a description of a series of qualitative
objectives (such as a mission statement). These will need to
be 'operationalized' (made quantitative) so that performance
against these objectives can be measured. Ultimately, objectives
are defined in terms of, for example, percentage turnover
growth on last year, improving operating profit from $y\%$ to $z\%$,
achieving market leadership in a defined market/segment, and
so on. There are two important points to note.

1 These objectives will be the basis for developing the strategic
direction of the organization and will involve the commitment
of corporate resources.

2 We must consider the objectives in the context of the market audit (i.e. the audit of the market environment within which the business operates, which we shall look at later in this chapter). Basically, we must assess how realistic the objectives are in terms of what is possible, given the market conditions. For example, it would be unrealistic for a small business with access to limited capital to set an objective to be the world market leader in building nuclear power stations within 12 months.

Business audit

The business audit is a review of the strengths and weaknesses of the business.

Examples of business strengths	Examples of business weaknesses
<ul><li>Market leadership</li><li>Some uniqueness as perceived by the customers (a differential advantage in terms of quality and/or price)</li><li>Control of a scarce resource related to differentiating our offering from that of the competition, e.g. access to a scarce resource (such as aggregates in construction), control of patents</li><li>A market-beating 'business process model' (i.e. how we organize our business), e.g. McDonald's, Lidl</li><li>Profitability</li><li>Brand loyalty</li></ul>	<ul><li>Low market share</li><li>No uniqueness perceived by the customers</li><li>Poor brand appeal</li><li>Poor business performance (lack of capital for reinvestment)</li><li>Poor employee morale</li></ul>

While in no way meant to be exhaustive, the following demonstrates the types of analysis undertaken during a business audit.

Business performance (last three years)

1 Sales and contribution by type of product/service
2 Sales and contribution by type of customer
3 Sales and contribution by geographical area
4 Top ten customer segments (profile)

Marketing mix

1 Product (width and depth of product range, features and benefits, product portfolio analysis)

2 Price (cost versus price, basis for pricing decisions)
3 Channels (channel selection and positioning)
4 Promotion (including current activities and budgets/spend levels, advertising, press relations, mail, outlets, personal selling, Internet)

Management knowledge

1 Perceptions of the company's strengths and weaknesses
2 Perceptions of customers' perceived needs (e.g. of value, price benefits)
3 Perceptions of the competition (market/segment shares, high profile accounts, capabilities in terms of strengths and weaknesses, geographical coverage, business objectives, policies, strategies, etc.)
4 Perceptions of the PEST environment in which the business operates

Market audit

This is a review of the **opportunities** and **threats** existing in the organization's business/market environment. There are two levels: the 'immediate' level and the 'general' level.

Immediate level

- **Customers** We have noted that customers/potential customers need to be segmented, i.e. placed into groups whose members share attitudes to product/service selection and differ from other segments within the same market.
- **Competitors** Perhaps surprisingly, companies embarking on a strategic marketing planning exercise often show a poor understanding of this group. We need to understand such issues as:
  - our competitors' recent 'track record' (business performance)
  - their declared corporate objectives/strategies
  - within segments, customers' perceptions of their offerings.
- **Intermediaries**
- **Suppliers**

General level

This level covers the PEST environment we have discussed previously.

- **Political** – e.g. prevailing political policies towards climate change
- **Economic** – e.g. level of growth in GNP, unemployment
- **Social** (or cultural) – e.g. society's attitudes to sustainability, energy conservation
- **Technological** – e.g. 'smartphone' technology

By combining the findings from the business audit and market audit, the marketer can assemble a **SWOT analysis** of strengths, weaknesses, opportunities and threats. This can be a powerful and very useful tool for developing the plan. One way to think about SWOT analysis is to consider it as a planning 'balance sheet': within the organization there will be strengths (+) and weaknesses (–), and in the marketplace there will be opportunities (+) and threats (–).

Within the organization	In the marketplace
Strengths +	Opportunities +
Weaknesses –	Threats –

The 'targeting' exercise
Targeting refers to deciding which segments the organization will select to focus on. It is the heart of the marketing planning

process and decisions made at this stage have a significant effect on the overall success of the plan. The task is to match the organization's strengths to opportunities in the marketplace so that the firm can obtain the best return on effort. There are two distinct tasks:

- to rank the market segments in terms of their attractiveness to the organization
- to rank the organization against the competition in terms of attractiveness to the market segments.

These two tasks can be represented in the following matrix.

Market/segment
attractiveness to the organization

	High	Low
High	1	2
Low	3	4

Organization's attractiveness to the market/ segments

The targeting matrix

- *Cell 1* This cell is the segment or segments that are highly attractive to the organization and to whose buyers the organization is highly attractive. This is the most effective matching of the organization to the segments.
- *Cell 2* Here the organization is still highly attractive to the segments but these segments are less attractive to the organization (they may be too small or offer poor creditworthiness). In this case the marketer may choose to 'sub-segment' the segments to isolate the most attractive parts that may be worth targeting.
- *Cell 3* While the segments are attractive to the organization, the segments do not perceive the organization to be attractive to them. In this case the marketer needs to assess

the basis of this perception. If our offering is objectively poorer than our competition, we must do something to address this disadvantage (e.g. improve product quality). However, if we can find no objective difference between our offering and that of our competitors, the problem is one of communication.

● *Cell 4* In this case the segments are unattractive to the organization and the organization is unattractive to the segments. Marketers 'de-target' (redirect resources *away* from these segments) in such circumstances.

The 'targeting' exercise normally produces a series of strategic options, i.e. actions that can be instituted in a number of segments either simultaneously or on a prioritized basis.

Marketing strategy

Establishing a successful marketing strategy involves deciding what to produce, how much to charge, where the customer will buy the product, and how to inform and persuade the customer to buy the product. Marketers have described this as the 'marketing mix' – product, price, place and promotion (i.e. the 4 Ps). We will look at the 4 Ps in more detail later in the week, but we can summarize each element here.

● **Product** This term encapsulates both tangible and intangible benefits carried by products and services. The product strategy must ensure that the firm's offering carries benefits that can be matched to customer needs.

● **Price** Prices must be set to reflect the benefits customers perceive in our offering compared to offerings from our competitors; i.e. which offers the best value.

● **Place** This term generally refers to channels of distribution, i.e. where the products are sold, including direct marketing channels such as the Internet.

● **Promotion** This is how we inform and communicate the benefits in our offering to the target market segments.

It involves developing messages and selecting the most cost-effective media to carry the messages to the target market segments. People will usually think of advertising (TV, radio, press, posters, etc.) and direct mail, but promotion also encompasses e-marketing (on the web) and public relations.

The marketer should draft separate marketing mixes (or marketing strategies) for each targeted segment, blending all the mix elements together to deliver satisfied customers and to meet the organization's stated marketing objectives.

Implementation

As we have already seen, the purpose of planning is to make our actions more effective. Planning without action is an arid academic exercise and of no real value to the organization. How the plan is implemented is therefore critical. Organizations often produce **tactical action plans** that:

1 set operational variables
2 establish time limits and deadlines
3 communicate and assign tasks
4 develop sales forecasts
5 determine action plans for individuals
6 prepare budgets.

Action plans need to be 'SMART' – specific, measurable, attainable, relevant and time bound.

Monitoring

Monitoring is a critical part of the planning process; only by using monitoring for control can we ensure that the strategy will achieve our objectives.

Not surprisingly, the first issue is monitoring the implementation of the plan in terms of achieving the stated objectives. In effect we are considering a loop that can be couched in a simple question: we have set measurable objectives but are we delivering to these objectives? We need to set appropriate timescales for monitoring and establish mechanisms to compare 'actual' to 'budget'. The purpose of this type of monitoring review is to ensure that the plan is 'on track' and, if not, to identify and make changes to ensure that we get it back on track. For some organizations, it is necessary to define the organization's objectives as 'milestones': what do we need to have achieved by the end of period 1 (to be defined by the organization) to be confident that we shall achieve our ultimate objective(s)?

In addition, the marketer needs to monitor the environment. Customers and competitors must be the main focus but general trends in the PEST environment must also be noted. We have seen that marketing research and the MkIS have an important role to play here. Where changes impact on the plan, action will be needed to respond to the changes so that they do not undermine its successful execution.

Effective marketing planning and the organization

At the beginning of the week we looked at the relationship between marketing and organizational performance and the body of evidence that suggests marketing is associated with improved profitability. However, there is also evidence that marketing planning does not always deliver improved performance, and research has been able to identify the following key requirements for the effective (and commercially successful) execution of marketing planning.

- **Ownership** It is important that those who have to implement the plan are given the opportunity to contribute to its development.
- **Rigour** The audit process (business and market) requires a significant amount of information, both from within the firm and from the marketplace. Lack of rigour in gathering, analysing and interpreting data can seriously undermine the effectiveness of the planning process. Marketers need to obtain thorough and objective information to reduce risk in decision making.

TIP

Modern IT systems and the planning process itself tend to produce a significant amount of information. Generally, 20 per cent of the information gathered accounts for 80 per cent of the information needed, so there is an additional need for selectivity.

- **Environmental sensitivity** Marketers must guard against trying to 'fit' the world outside to the plan. Change is endemic to all market situations, and planning processes must be reviewed in the light of the changing environment. Organizations must be environmentally sensitive and have the flexibility to be able to respond to changes, both opportunities and threats.
- **Company-wide appreciation** All employees need to appreciate the broad issues involved in the plan so that they can contribute to its success (i.e. share the same agendas as other staff).
- **Management belief** Senior management must believe that the process of planning will reduce risk in decision making and contribute to the success of the business. Without this belief, the process can easily lose staff enthusiasm and rigour and ultimately become a pointless bureaucratic exercise marginalized in the business.

Alternative approaches

The marketing decision process described above is used, in different formats, by a wide range of organizations, both large and small, manufacturing and services and for profit and not-for-profit. In addition, marketing consultants often use this approach when supporting clients in improving the benefits they can derive from marketing planning.

However, there are a number of other approaches to managing the strategic direction of a business. Among them are the Boston Box, the Ansoff Box and Porter's Three Generic Strategies.

The Boston Box

Larger organizations often face the problem of managing their portfolio of products (all the products they offer to the marketplace). It is important that the organization's resources support those products that offer the best return on investment. One famous approach to analysing this problem is known as the Boston Box.

Relative market share

	High	Low
High	Star	Problem child
Low	Cash cow	Dog

(Market growth rate)

The Boston Box

Source: Boston Consulting Group

The Boston Box classifies products in terms of two variables: relative market share and market growth rate.

Star These products are in high growth markets and the organization has a high relative (to the competition) market share. These products often need high investment to maintain their market position but may become 'cash cows'.

Cash cow These are low-growth, high market share products. They are established and successful, have low investment needs and produce a positive cash flow.

Problem child These products are in high growth markets but have low relative market share. They require investment to maintain (let alone increase) market share and marketers have to decide whether these products will succeed or fail.

Dog These products are low growth, low market share. They may generate enough cash to maintain themselves but do not offer any medium/long-term potential for the organization.

Balancing the portfolio

Organizations must balance their product portfolios: too many of any one type can create major problems. Even too many 'cash cows', which would seem like the best situation for an organization, cause a problem – markets are dynamic and the current demand for cash cows will eventually decline. The organization needs 'stars' to replace the current 'cash cows' in the future.

The Ansoff Box

An alternative way to look at the organization's relationship with its customers is to study the relationship between products and customers. Igor Ansoff created another famous tool, often referred to as the Ansoff Box, which looked at an organization's product mix in terms of the relationship between existing and new products and existing and new customers. The Ansoff Box ranks the best return on effort in the short term based on four product/customer relationships.

	Customer	
	Existing	New
Product Existing	1	3
Product New	2	4

The Ansoff Box

Source: H. Igor Ansoff, *Corporate Strategy* (Harmondsworth: Penguin, 1965)

The numbers in the cells represent the ranking of each product/customer relationship and identify that selling existing products to existing customers offers the best return on effort in the short term. However, selling 'new' (i.e. new to the customers) products to existing customers offers the second-best return on effort in the short term.

Porter's Three Generic Strategies

In his book *Competitive Strategy*, Michael Porter developed the concept of the Three Generic Strategies for outperforming other businesses in an industry.

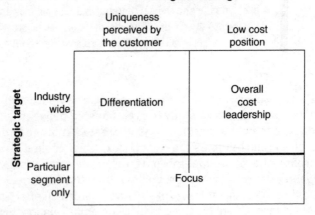

Three Generic Strategies

Source: Michael E. Porter, *Competitive Strategy* (Free Press, 1998)

Overall cost leadership Here emphasis is on cost minimization and control, so the business can still earn returns after its competitors have competed away their profits through rivalry.

Differentiation Here management seeks to differentiate the product or service by creating something that is perceived industry wide to be unique: perhaps through brand, technological advantages, patents or control of scarce resources.

Focus The management focus here is on a particular buyer group and seeks to serve that target particularly well, through either uniqueness perceived by the customer or low cost.

Porter's Three Generic Strategies are viable approaches for dealing with competitive forces. However, a business failing to develop its strategy in at least one of the three directions – a 'stuck in the middle' firm – is in an extremely poor strategic situation and is almost guaranteed low profitability.

Summary

Marketing planning is a strategic activity – marketers have to make a range of decisions that translate into actions in the future to achieve their objectives. It is a decision process that focuses on matching the strengths of the organization to market opportunities and creating detailed action plans designed to deliver the organization's objectives.

The steps involved in market planning are:

1 setting objectives
2 reviewing the strengths and weaknesses of the organization (through a business audit)
3 assessing the opportunities and threats in the marketplace (through a market audit)
4 conducting a 'targeting' exercise that matches the strengths of the organization to opportunities presented by different market segments
5 developing an integrated marketing strategy (marketing mix)
6 implementing and controlling the execution of the strategy to meet the organization's objectives.

Marketing planning is a key strategic link between the organization and its marketplace and plays a vital part in the successful management of a business.

SUNDAY
MONDAY
TUESDAY
WEDNESDAY
THURSDAY
FRIDAY
SATURDAY

Fact-check (answers at the back)

1. What is marketing planning?
   a) A strategic activity ❏
   b) A gift some businesspeople are born with ❏
   c) A skill you can only learn from a business school ❏
   d) A technique only management consultants use ❏

2. What does the marketing planning process start with?
   a) Advertising ❏
   b) Selling ❏
   c) Setting objectives ❏
   d) Retailing ❏

3. What does the business audit review?
   a) Economic climate ❏
   b) Strengths and weaknesses of the organization ❏
   c) Trends in social attitudes ❏
   d) Competition ❏

4. What does the market audit review?
   a) Opportunities and threats in the business/market environment ❏
   b) Skills in our organization ❏
   c) Our sales growth over the last three financial years ❏
   d) Our operating profit over the last three financial years ❏

5. What does the 'targeting' exercise help marketers do?
   a) Decide which segments the organization will focus on ❏
   b) Check if the plan is going to be effective ❏
   c) Win prizes in business competitions ❏
   d) Respond positively to journalists' requests for information ❏

6. The marketing mix involves decisions regarding what?
   a) Rebates, rates, revisions and returns ❏
   b) Product, price, place and promotion ❏
   c) Scales, summaries, shifts and scenarios ❏
   d) Training, timetables, tokens and tolls ❏

7. What is the purpose of monitoring?
   a) To ensure that the plan achieves the stated objectives ❏
   b) To check that employees are doing their jobs ❏
   c) To decide who will receive bonuses ❏
   d) None of the above ❏

8. What is the Boston Box based on?
a) Making sure that the product's packaging meets customers' needs ❏
b) Improving the in-house flow of information ❏
c) Preventing competitors discovering our strategy ❏
d) Relative market share and market growth rate ❏

9. What is the Ansoff Box based on?
a) The relationship between existing and new customers and existing and new products ❏
b) Relative market share and market growth rate ❏
c) The critical mass of markets and segments ❏
d) None of the above ❏

10. What are Porter's Three Generic Strategies?
a) Processes, solutions and testing ❏
b) Leadership, motivation and remuneration ❏
c) Production, selling and marketing ❏
d) Overall cost leadership, differentiation and focus ❏

The marketing mix – product and price

Yesterday we looked at marketing planning and introduced the idea of developing an integrated marketing strategy, the marketing mix. We saw that a successful marketing strategy involves deciding what to produce, how much to charge, where the customer will buy the product, and how to inform and persuade the customer to buy the product using the 4 Ps: product, price, place and promotion.

In this and the following chapters we are going to look at each of these four elements of the marketing mix in more detail.

Today we are going to look at *product* and *price*. We will consider tangible and intangible product benefits, explore the differences between products and services, and review the relationship between product features and benefits. We will then go on to discuss brands, the product life cycle, new product development and product strategy decisions.

Three forces act on pricing – the target audience's perception of value in our and competitors' offerings, our cost structure and the competition's price levels. We will look at these before considering some key issues of pricing strategy decisions.

Product

'Product' is the fundamental basis of the marketing mix. Our 'product' carries benefits that satisfy customers' needs and, while it can be a tangible, physical entity, 'product' can also be something quite intangible such as a service, an experience or an idea. In the context of the marketing mix, we can define 'product' as follows.

> **'A product is anything that is offered to the marketplace that can satisfy a customer's perceived need.'**

Our **product strategy** is the method by which we **satisfy** customers' needs. Here we are going to look at the factors affecting our product strategy: tangible and intangible benefits; the differences between products and services; features and benefits; brands; the product life cycle; new product development; and product strategy decisions.

Tangible and intangible benefits

A product can be tangible or intangible. Some writers have tried to establish a tangible–intangible continuum, with highly tangible products at one extreme (e.g. salt) and highly intangible products at the other extreme (e.g. insurance).

Tangible	**Intangible**
←——————————————————————→	
Salt	Insurance

The tangible–intangible continuum

It's probably accurate to say that most offerings have some element of tangible and intangible benefits as part of their appeal. Let's look at some examples.

- **Cars** The physical nature of the product has a high element of tangibility, but there are intangible benefits such as the brand and dealer service.

- **Personal computers** Again, these have a high element of physical product, but aspects such as brand and pre- and post-service support add intangible benefits.
- **Restaurants** The food is tangible but the overall benefit is made up of intangibles like the decor, the ambience, the service and the restaurant's reputation.
- **Perfumes** The core offering is intangible in terms of the benefits customers derive from the purchase but the offering is 'delivered' as a tangible product.

Differences between products and services

Given that most offerings have some element of tangible and intangible benefits as part of their appeal, it is still possible to distinguish **products** (i.e. with a high degree of tangibility) from **services** (i.e. with a high degree of intangibility). There are five key differences between products and services:

- **Heterogeneity** Services can usually be designed around a specific requirement: a consultancy assignment can be designed to meet one client's unique needs. Products tend to be more homogeneous: for volume car producers one can only select from the specifications on offer.
- **Intangibility** As we've seen, products with a high tangible element can be touched, tasted and taken apart to examine how they work; there is a 'trial' element. Services do not have this trial element.
- **Inseparability** The production of a service and its consumption occur at the same time: there is a direct link between provider and customer. The production and consumption of highly tangible products, on the other hand, are separate.
- **Perishableness** Unlike products, services cannot be stocked or held over. A hotel bedroom that is not occupied on a particular night is a revenue opportunity lost.
- **Lack of ownership** Access to or use of a service facility does not mean the customer obtains ownership. The purchase is often time related, e.g. a hotel room reservation for three nights.

Features and benefits

Whether predominately tangible or intangible, a product must carry benefits that satisfy customers' needs. **Benefits** are those elements of the product that meet customers' needs (as discussed on Monday). **Features** carry benefits.

It is important to differentiate between a benefit and a feature. Telling a customer about a feature may not enable him/her to understand how the product meets his/her perceived needs. Features are the product's capabilities; benefits are the outcomes customers 'consume' by way of meeting their perceived needs.

Features carry benefits

Let's consider an example. Many cars today have antilock braking systems (ABS) as standard. ABS is not a benefit per se but a feature that carries a benefit that fulfils a need.

- Feature: ABS
- Benefit: safer braking
- Need: safety

Customers don't care about features unless they're experienced in buying the specific type of product we are offering. For example, when personal computers (PCs) were first marketed to individuals and Small Office Home Office (SoHo) users, the promotional emphasis was on technical performance features, such as RAM, hard disc size and CPU speed. Many potential customers were put off by the 'jargon' because they could not see what benefits these features would offer to them. In essence, they asked, 'What's in it for me?' Most people now understand these terms and can judge the benefits in an offering from a list of features. In effect, the features list can become a type of shorthand between the experienced customer and the producer.

> *When presenting a customer with a benefit, the marketer can use a feature as evidence that the benefit exists. Our ABS example demonstrates this point well.*

Brands

An important form of intangible benefit is the **brand**. A brand is a name, term, sign, symbol, association, trademark or design which is intended to identify the products or services of one provider or group of providers, and to differentiate them from those of competitors.

Customers develop loyalty to a brand, based on previous experience if they have purchased the product before and found that it has met their perceived needs. Alternatively, a brand can be associated with a lifestyle or particular condition that is important to the customer and that they aspire to.

In addition, brands can add value to a product: for instance, many customers would perceive a bottle of Chanel perfume as a high-quality, exclusive and expensive product. But the same fragrance in an unmarked bottle would probably be viewed as lower quality even if the two fragrances were identical. Some commentators have cited this as an example of marketers taking advantage of customers, but the intangible benefits the customer obtains from the brand meet important needs such as self-actualization and the esteem of others.

Brand extension

Although the Chanel brand started as a French fashion house, the product range now includes fragrances, fine jewellery and watches, leather goods and shoes, and even eyewear and sporting goods. This is known as brand extension – the application of a brand beyond its initial range of products or outside its category. This becomes possible when the brand image has contributed to a perception with the consumer/user, where brand and not product is the decision driver.

From the marketer's perspective, brand management seeks to make the product or services relevant to the target segments. Brands should be seen as more than the difference between the actual cost of a product and its selling price: brands represent the sum of all valuable qualities of a product to the customer. It follows that marketers must be careful not to allow anything to damage the brand's reputation. For example, when the presence of the chemical benzene was found in a small sample of bottles of Perrier water in the USA in 1990, Perrier voluntarily recalled its entire inventory of Perrier from store shelves throughout the United States. This action demonstrated to the market the importance Perrier placed on the quality of their product and their commitment to deal with any problem quickly and thoroughly – to do whatever was necessary to protect the integrity of the brand.

The product life cycle

Most products display similar characteristics to living organisms – they are 'born', grow to maturity, decline and 'die'. They have a product life cycle (PLC). For example, the stand-alone facsimile (fax) machine was launched in the 1970s and was adopted by a wide range of organizations and individuals during the 1980s. However, the spread of Internet access, email and scanning had a major impact on the sales of fax machines.

While the life expectancy of products varies greatly, most products go through four stages: introduction, growth, maturity and decline, as shown graphically below.

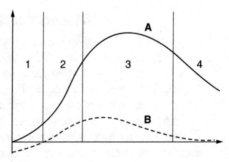

The product life cycle

The horizontal axis of the graph represents time and the vertical axis represents sales (depicted by graph line A) and profit (depicted by graph line B). We can consider some of the properties of the four stages.

1 Introduction

At this stage the product has been introduced to the market, sales growth is slow and profits are negative due to the costs of launch. A particular group of buyers is adopting the new product. These are known as 'innovators' and are characterized by their desire for new experiences and a relatively high degree of risk taking. As a marketing rule of thumb, this group accounts for around 10 per cent of the market.

2 Growth

If the product is perceived to have benefits matched to customers' needs, it will become more widely adopted. Sales will grow quickly and profits will follow suit. The growth stage is driven by a group of buyers known as 'early adopters' who have an appetite for new (and better) solutions to their needs but who lack the risk taking of the innovators. This group generally accounts for around 20 per cent of the market.

3 Maturity

At some point the product's sales growth will slow and it will enter its mature stage. Commonly the longest period, sales and profits peak during the maturity stage. This stage is characterized by the adoption of the product by the majority of the market, known as the 'late adopters'. This group accounts for around 60 per cent of the market.

4 Decline

Eventually, the product's sales are likely to decline. This can be due to new products being seen as a better match to customers' needs, changing customers' attitudes or increased competition. Even during this stage, new customers are adopting the product. These 'laggards' can be characterized by a generally conservative outlook and a low threshold to risk. This group accounts for around 10 per cent of the market.

The marketer will obviously face different strategic issues for each stage of the PLC and may have a portfolio of products at different stages. It is worth noting the relationship between the PLC concept and the Boston Box we looked at on Wednesday. In simple terms we can align the two as shown below.

PLC	Boston Box
Introduction	Problem child
Growth	Star
Maturity	Cash cow
Decline	Dog

New product development

Customers change and the PEST factors change and exert an influence on customers. Consequently, the marketer must be alert to the need for new solutions to customers' needs. **New product development (NPD)** is therefore an important element of the organization's product strategy. New products cost an organization until they reach growth stage and some products do not achieve this stage and fail, with the resultant impact on the organization's profitability. The marketer needs to maximize the chances of a new product becoming established (i.e. reaching maturity in PLC terms or becoming a 'cash cow' in Boston Box terms). NPD success is linked to the **diffusion of innovation**, i.e. the way new ideas or products are communicated through certain channels over time to a marketplace. Several factors determine whether and how quickly an innovation will be adopted.

- **Relative advantage** Potential adopters must perceive that the innovation is an improvement over the previous solution to their needs. In some NPD situations, the customer has a poorly defined need because there had been no solution to their needs up to that point. This is the 'anticipation' element of our definition of marketing.
- **Compatibility** Potential adopters must perceive the innovation as being consistent with their existing values, past experiences and needs. An idea that is incompatible with their values and norms will either not be adopted at all or not be adopted as rapidly as an innovation that is compatible.

- **Relative complexity/simplicity** If the innovation is too difficult to understand or use, it is less likely to be adopted.
- **Trialability** If the potential adopter may try or experiment with the innovation, this will increase the chances of it being adopted.
- **Observability** The more easily an innovation is visible to others, the more this will drive communication among peers and personal networks. In turn this will create more positive or negative reactions (i.e. the effect of 'innovators' on 'early adopters').

Product strategy decisions

Marketers have to make a series of decisions regarding the product offering. We can summarize these decisions under four headings.

1 **Core benefit** As we have seen, the product must carry benefits to meet the customers' perceived needs. In general terms the marketer needs to understand the hierarchy of needs (the relative importance of customers' perceived needs) and ensure that the product carries benefits (tangible and intangible) matched to these needs.

2 **Actual product** Decisions in this area include product design, styling, quality, colours, branding and packaging. In effect this is the manifestation of the core benefits.

3 **Augmented product** Decisions in this area involve anything that can add value to the customer (and differentiate our offering from that of the competition) and could include installation, warranty, credit facilities and after-sales service.

4 **Product range (depth and width)** Decisions in this area involve the 'width' of the product range (e.g. small family hatchback, family saloon car, executive saloon car) and the 'depth' (e.g. range of engines on offer, trim levels, equipment levels).

For companies to ensure continued evolution, they must define their industries broadly to take advantage of growth opportunities. They must ascertain and act on their customers' needs and desires, not bank on the presumed longevity of their products. An organization must learn to think of itself not as producing goods or services but as doing the things that will make people want to do business with it.

Price

This is the second part of the marketing mix and, while all parts of the mix are inextricably linked, there is a particularly strong link between the product and price parts of it. At its basic level, price is the amount a customer must pay to obtain the benefit(s) from a product or service – the **exchange** we referred to on Sunday.

In considering price strategy, we are going to look at the three interrelated forces acting on any organization's decisions regarding pricing (the '**pricing triangle**') and pricing strategy decisions:

● the target audience's perception of value in our and the competition's offerings
● our cost structure
● the competition's price levels.

We can represent this interrelationship as the pricing triangle.

The pricing triangle

The target audience's perception of value

Value is the customer's perception of the match of benefits in an offering to their needs and is measured by the customer's willingness to pay for it. We can illustrate this with a simple example: a customer sees three products (A, B and C) as having *exactly the same* benefits matched to his/her needs. However, the products have different prices.

Product	Price
A	225.00
B	264.00
C	210.00

In this situation the product with the lowest price (i.e. product C) offers the best value, i.e. the most benefits at the lowest cost. We can present this as a simple equation:

$$Value = \frac{Benefits}{Price}$$

Many of us will be familiar with the process of deciding on a particular make and model of a product and searching for the lowest price supplier.

However, if the three products are perceived to have *different* bundles of benefits, the job of assessing the value in each product is made more difficult for the customer. Customers adopt a range of strategies to deal with this situation. Some do a thorough analysis of the benefits offered by the competing products and calculate the best value on this basis. Others will focus on just one or two of their most important perceived needs and decide on that basis. Others will rely on their experiences of particular brands, while some will always choose the lowest price option, regardless of the benefits on offer.

Consumer durables (products such as cars and washing machines) and many products purchased by organizations have an added value component of **cost over time**. For instance, an airline company will be interested not only in the purchase price of an aeroplane but the running cost over time. It may include issues such as taxes on carbon emissions.

Price can also be inextricably linked to the customers' perception of quality and hence value. With a luxury brand such as Chanel, if the product were 'too cheap' it would be difficult for the customer to accept that the benefits they perceive in the product can be obtained for such a 'low' price. This phenomenon is known as '**customer dissonance**' and further illustrates the link between product and pricing strategies.

Quality and price

The Belgian brewer Stella Artois ran a promotional campaign in the UK between 1982 and 2007 using the slogan 'Reassuringly expensive'. The intention was to make the relatively high price of the product a benefit rather than a barrier and take advantage of the consumer linking quality with price.

Our cost structure

Price and cost are not the same. Price is ultimately controlled by customers' value perceptions; cost is the monetary value of producing and delivering the product, including profit. We need to define costs, which fall into two broad groups.

- **Variable costs** are so called because they vary directly with the level of production – the more we produce, the more variable costs we incur. Examples are raw materials, labour and operating expenses directly related to production.
- **Fixed costs,** also known as overheads, do not vary with the level of production. Whether we make anything or not, we will still incur these costs. Examples are office/factory rent, business rates and salaries of sales staff and management.

At a certain level of units of production (and hence revenue), the total cost (fixed and variable) matches the revenue value. This is known as the **breakeven point**: as production increases from this point, the organization will make profits.

From the marketer's perspective, cost sets the limit to the low end of pricing. The following table considers six scenarios (A–F) of differing relationships of the key variables of units of production, which are number of units, unit price, revenue (units of production x unit price), variable cost (VC) per unit, VC per unit x units of production, fixed cost (FC) and profit/loss.

| | Scenario | | | | | |
	A	B	C	D	E	F
Units number	5,000	5,000	5,000	15,000	5,000	20,000
Unit price £	10	20	10	10	10	10
Revenue (units × unit price) £	50,000	100,000	50,000	150,000	50,000	200,000
VC per unit £	4	4	8	8	10.5	10.5
VC per unit × units £	20,000	20,000	40,000	120,000	52,500	210,000
FC £	30,000	30,000	30,000	30,000	30,000	30,000
Profit/loss £	0	50,000	−20,000	0	−32,500	−40,000

A This is an example of the simple breakeven position. In this scenario 5,000 units at a selling price of £10.00, a variable cost (VC) per unit of £4.00 and fixed costs (FC) of £30,000 will yield breakeven.

B In this scenario the price is double that of scenario A while all other factors remain the same. In this case the organization would deliver a profit of £50,000. This example demonstrates the effect on the 'bottom line' of increasing price levels.

C This scenario is the same as A apart from increased variable costs (up from £4.00 per unit to £8.00) and this yields a loss of £20,000.

D This is the breakeven position based on the costs in scenario C. The units of output need to triple (from 5,000 to 15,000). This demonstrates that, when the difference (known as the 'contribution') between the selling price and the variable cost is relatively low (£2.00 in this case), units of output have to increase significantly to achieve breakeven.

E This scenario is the same as A but with increased variable costs (up from £4.00 per unit to £10.50), £0.50 *more* than selling price. This scenario yields a loss of £32,500.

F In this scenario units of output have quadrupled but losses have increased (from £32,500 to £40,000). This demonstrates that increasing output will only worsen the organization's losses when variable costs are *above* selling price.

The competition's price levels

This is the third point of our pricing triangle. We can do everything we can to understand our customers' needs, match benefits to needs and try to give the customer the best value proposition, but we mustn't forget that our competitors will be doing the same.

Some products are difficult to differentiate from one another – such as nails and screws (fixings) and petrol – and with these the lowest price strategy will win.

Different approaches

Organizations adopt different approaches to pricing. For instance, the US retailer Walmart (Asda in the UK) bases its strategic positioning on being the lowest price provider in a broad industry sector. BMW, on the other hand, seeks to differentiate its offer across a range of market segments and it bases its product pricing on customers' perceptions of the value they see in the BMW brand. Chanel adopts the focus approach, targeting particular market segments and differentiating its offering through its exclusivity.

In many organizations pricing offers the marketer the most immediate and flexible tool in the marketing mix because it is relatively easy to change prices. Consequently, many organizations rely on price cuts to generate sales or to meet a competitive threat. But this may be a 'double-edged sword': although a price cut may generate sales in the short term, it may undermine the customers' perceptions of the value of the product. Price-cut sales promotions seem to promise two important benefits:

- they generate increased sales volume
- they induce non-buyers to trial and then perhaps become regular customers.

We can consider each in turn.

- It is true that temporary price promotions do generate a sales 'spike'. However, research by Ehrenberg, Hammond & Goodhardt (1994) suggests that around 80 per cent of the people who buy a brand on a price promotion deal already use the brand anyway and the company has a reduced margin on these sales. Sales volume is one thing but profitability is quite another.
- Ehrenberg *et al.* demonstrated that there is no long-term effect on loyalty/repeat buying rates from price-related sales promotions. Where customers 'brand switch' in line with the promotion, they return to their original brand when the price promotion is lifted.

To be effective, the marketer must remain vigilant and aware of not only what the competitors are doing but, equally importantly, what customers are thinking and doing with regard to their offering and that of their competitors. This underlines the importance of marketing information and research.

Pricing strategy decisions

Pricing decisions must take into account the three forces described in the pricing triangle above. However, price is also part of the overall marketing mix and interrelated with the other parts of the mix. If we choose to operate in an undifferentiated market (e.g. petrol retailing), our pricing strategy will reflect the fact that it is difficult to differentiate our offering from that of the competition in terms of additional benefits matched to customers' needs. On the other hand, if we operate in the luxury goods market (e.g. fragrances, fine jewellery, watches), we can expect to be able to use our benefits (including intangibles such as brand) to differentiate our offering from that of the competition. Products and services must therefore be 'price positioned' so that:

● the customer perceives the value in the offering
● the customer perceives our offering to be better value than that of the competition
● we are able to make a profit (defined here as the surplus after subtracting total costs from total revenue) in the medium term.

Time and pricing

Time is an additional variable to consider. The product life cycle demonstrates the link between units purchased (revenue) and time. When a new product is launched, some organizations choose to set a high price. This is called **market-skimming pricing**. As the product moves into the mature stage, prices can be reduced to stimulate increased adoption. This is known as **market-penetration pricing**.

Summary

Today we focused on two parts of the marketing mix: product and price.

Product is anything that satisfies a customer's perceived needs, and involves both tangible and intangible elements. Services tend to be more intangible than products. Features are a product's capabilities and carry benefits, which may be tangible (such as safer braking) or intangible (such as brand).

The product life cycle is introduction–growth–maturity–decline. Although new product development is expensive, finding new solutions to changing customer needs is vital.

Three forces influence pricing: audience perception of value, cost structure and competitors' prices. A key concept is value – benefits against price. When all offerings carry the same benefits, the lowest price offering represents the best value.

Cost is not the same as price but is the monetary value of profitable production/delivery and includes fixed and variable elements.

SUNDAY
MONDAY
TUESDAY
WEDNESDAY
THURSDAY
FRIDAY
SATURDAY

Fact-check (answers at the back)

1. What is a product ?
   a) The outcome of customers'
      spending ❏
   b) The motive driving
      customers' needs ❏
   c) The end result of a purchase ❏
   d) The fundamental basis
      of the marketing mix ❏

2. Do products have either
   intangible or tangible
   benefits, but not both?
   a) Yes, that's correct ❏
   b) Only for services ❏
   c) No, products can have
      both intangible and tangible
      benefits ❏
   d) Only for luxury food products ❏

3. What is a product feature?
   a) The basis for an advertising
      campaign ❏
   b) The product's capabilities
      that carry benefits to
      customers' needs ❏
   c) The best aspect of a product ❏
   d) An article in a magazine
      about a new product ❏

4. What is a brand?
   a) The packaging ❏
   b) The theme for an
      advertising campaign ❏
   c) A new product idea ❏
   d) An important form of
      intangible benefit ❏

5. What is the growth and
   subsequent decline in a
   product's revenue over
   time known as?
   a) Product life cycle ❏
   b) Product trajectory ❏
   c) Product roller coaster ❏
   d) Product big dipper ❏

6. What is new product
   development (NPD)
   success linked to?
   a) The diffusion of innovation ❏
   b) The advertising budget ❏
   c) The product's time in
      development ❏
   d) The time of year it is
      launched ❏

7. What does Levitt's concept
   of 'marketing myopia' say?
   a) Customers do not see all
      the products available
      to them ❏
   b) Customers do not see all
      advertisements ❏
   c) Marketers cannot see
      all the potential customers
      in the market ❏
   d) Organizations must be
      customer oriented rather
      than product oriented ❏

8. What is price?
a) What it costs to make a product ❏
b) The printed price before you start haggling ❏
c) The amount a customer must pay to obtain the benefits from a product or service ❏
d) Always set to be 10% lower than the competition ❏

9. What is the value equation?
a) Needs/benefits ❏
b) Tangible benefits/intangible benefits ❏
c) Price/cost ❏
d) Benefits/price ❏

10. What are total costs made up of?
a) Prices and costs ❏
b) Variable and fixed costs ❏
c) New and existing costs ❏
d) None of the above ❏

FRIDAY

The marketing mix – place

Yesterday we focused on the first two parts of the marketing mix – product and price. Today we are going to focus on the *place* part of the mix, the third of the 4 Ps.

In its simplest terms and probably original sense, place is where the 'exchange' (of product or service for the price) takes place. The term marketplace can conjure up images of stalls in open market squares, bazaars and souqs and, as we said at the beginning of the week, marketing began with this fundamental relationship between buyers and sellers. In the modern context, however, place focuses on how products and services are distributed to customers.

Today we will look at channels of distribution, types of channels, channel characteristics and some of the key issues in decisions related to distribution channel strategy.

Place and distribution

In the modern context the 'place' part of the marketing mix focuses on how products and services are distributed to customers. This **distribution** may refer to the physical distribution of products or the channels of distribution.

- **Physical distribution** is the *planning, monitoring and control of the distribution and delivery of manufactured goods* and forms an important part of ensuring that the product is available to customers in the quantities required at the time they want to buy.
- **Channels of distribution** are the third parties that make the product or service available for use or consumption by the customer.

We can imagine a simple channel of distribution as follows:

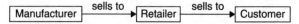

In our example, if a manufacturer uses a retailer, then the retailer must add a cost to the manufacturer's price. For this to make business sense, the retailer must **add value** to the marketing process. Retailers, or intermediaries in general, can add value in a number of ways.

- Dealing with a small number of retailers is more **economical** for the manufacturer than dealing directly with a large number of end customers.

- Retailers will take much **larger volumes** of products than end customers and this offers cost savings to the manufacturer in terms of physical delivery.
- The **location** of retail premises meets customers' buying behaviour, e.g. in out-of-town shopping centres.
- For some goods, the **reputation** of the retailer can enhance the product's perceived value, e.g. Harrods.

It is probably easier to think of channels of distribution in the context of products than of services because, as we have seen, 'inseparability' is a characteristic of services (its production and consumption occur at the same time). However, services can be delivered through intermediaries too. Examples are travel agents and mortgage brokers.

The channel relationship should provide a mutual benefit to the manufacturer/service provider and the intermediary.

Channel types

There are two broad types of distribution channel available to the marketer: intermediaries and direct.

Intermediaries

Intermediaries are independent organizations that carry out a number of activities associated with adding value to the marketing process. The two main groups are retailers and wholesalers.

Retailers include organizations such as:

- supermarkets (Tesco, Sainsburys)
- department stores (House of Fraser, John Lewis Partnership)
- high street chains (Topshop, Next)
- convenience store groups (Martin McColl, Spar)
- independent retailers, including speciality stores
- franchises (McDonald's, IKEA, Subway).

Wholesalers primarily sell goods and services to those buying for resale and/or business use. They include:

● wholesale merchants – sell primarily to retailers and can be general (i.e. sell a range of products, e.g. Booker Wholesale) or specialist (i.e. fish wholesalers, e.g. M&J Seafood, part of the Brakes Group)
● cash-and-carry wholesalers – sell from fixed premises and do not normally deliver; buyers come to them for their requirements (e.g. Selco Builders' Warehouse)
● industrial distributors – sell to manufacturers rather than retailers and can carry a range of stock to meet customers' needs (e.g. Nationwide Fuels who supply a range of industrial lubricants to industry in the UK)
● producers' co-operatives – are prevalent in the agricultural market; members assemble groups of products to be sold to customers and share the profits.

Direct channels

Organizations often choose to trade directly with customers because of cost issues but also because of the potential for building customer relations. Direct channels can be broadly divided into two groups: traditional and new media.

Traditional channels

These are 'traditional' in the sense that they have been used for some time. The following are some of the best-known examples.

- Direct mail – involves posting promotional material direct to the potential customers' home or office and encouraging customers to buy direct (e.g. Readers' Digest).
- Catalogue-based home shopping – is a variant of direct mail, where a catalogue is forwarded to the customer and they are encouraged to purchase products represented in the catalogue (e.g. Littlewoods catalogue).
- Inserts – are promotional material placed in selected magazines with instructions for buying direct.
- Telemarketing – uses the telephone to sell directly to customers in both consumer and B2B markets.
- Direct selling – includes door-to-door selling and party plan (e.g. Party Plan UK) in consumer markets.
- Personal selling –can include own salaried staff and/or sales agents. Sales forces are common in B2B markets where there is a strong benefit from personal relationships between the salesperson and the buyer.
- TV shopping – is more accurately known as direct response television marketing (DRTV). DRTV is common in the US and now more widespread in other markets such as the UK following the proliferation of satellite and free-to-air channels. DRTV involves the direct promotion of a product to the audience and typically a freephone number for them to make their purchase.

New media

The explosion of digital-based technology has opened up a wide range of new channels for marketers. Of major use in promotion (which we will discuss tomorrow), new media also offer additional channels of distribution.

- Websites – are widely used by all sorts of organizations and individuals and have been described as 'online shop windows'. Clearly, with the addition of e-commerce (the transactional element), organizations can trade directly with their customers, opening a new channel. Many organizations have traditional retail channels but also trade direct from their websites.
- Specialist sites – e.g. eBay have a seller development team committed to helping sellers grow their business within the eBay channel.

- E-direct mail – is used in the same way as traditional direct mail but using email to communicate a particular message or to direct the recipient to a website.
- Mobile phone marketing – has been made possible by the growth in ownership of smartphones and 3G/4G networks and associated software so customers can purchase through their mobile phone.
- Podcasts and vodcasts – are audio and video (respectively) files that can be downloaded to a mobile device. Marketers are experimenting with different approaches to using these technologies as effective channels.

Changing channels

One important component of distribution channels is **change**. As with the influence of change on the marketing process, decisions related to distribution channels are no different. Channels are subject to similar PEST and market forces as products, and over time different channels grow and then decline in a way that resembles the product life cycle.

Traditional channels are making way for new media channels, and one major change has been the Internet share of retailing. The chart below shows the Internet share in percentage terms of the average weekly value of all retailing in the UK in the period 2006–11.

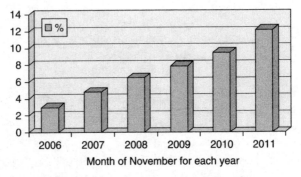

Month of November for each year

Internet share (%) of average weekly value for all retailing in UK
Source: Retail sales – November 2011: Office for National Statistics, UK

These data show the significant growth (up from 3 per cent in 2006 to 12.2 per cent in 2011) in market share obtained by Internet-based retailing out of all UK retailing. Perhaps one of the best-known Internet retailers is Amazon.com. The business was incorporated in 1994 and trades in the USA and a number of other countries in Europe and Asia. Net sales in the year to 31 December 2010 were $34.2 billion, up 319 per cent on 2006 (sales in 2006 being $10.7 billion).

Channel characteristics

The type and nature of channel relationships are based on an agreement between the parties involved and can be quite diverse. To take a simple manufacturer/retailer example, this could be a medium-term contractual relationship or a more informal, flexible relationship.

Some producers establish exclusive channels; car manufacturers, for example, have 'dealer networks'. In this case there is a much stronger 'partnering' theme to the relationship than there would be in a less formal manufacturer/retailer relationship. Dealers agree to invest in their business in support of the investment of their manufacturer partner, and manufacturers commit to supporting their dealers through promotions and so on.

The relative 'power' of the players in a distribution channel can vary quite significantly. For instance, in our example of the car manufacturer and dealer, one might say there is a 'symbiotic' (mutually advantageous) relationship. However, in different markets different members of the channel can have significantly more 'power' than the other members. Two extreme examples of this '**channel captaincy**' are:

- **UK supermarkets** Keynote estimates that Tesco, ASDA, Sainsbury's and Morrisons, followed by Waitrose, Aldi, Lidl and Marks & Spencer, accounted for around 93 per cent of retail food sales in the UK in 2009. This places the large supermarkets in an extremely strong bargaining position with their suppliers.
- **luxury goods** With luxury goods the manufacturer selects the retailer and gives that retailer an exclusive territory, agreeing

not to sell to any other retailer in a designated area. Rolex, the luxury watch manufacturer, operates in this way. Its 'dealer locator' page on their website enables customers to identify where they can buy Rolex watches in a particular area. The strength of the brand gives the manufacturer the power to select retailers and negotiate terms.

While channel members depend on one another, they often act alone in their own short-term best interests. Maintaining a mutually beneficial relationship can therefore be difficult. Clearly, the greater the investment and the longer the contractual relationship, the more likely it is that channel members can operate in a mutually beneficial way.

Distribution channel strategy decisions

As with all aspects of marketing, the starting point must be the organization's target customer segments. They must ask two key questions.

- Does the channel put the product in the right place: where the target customer wants to buy it?
- Does the channel add value?

Marketers often consider the channels their competition utilizes and may choose to be in the same channel so that customers see their product at the same time as they see their competitors'. For example, a proprietary food brand might want to be in the same supermarkets as their direct competitors. Alternatively, marketers may wish (or be forced) to adopt different channels from their competitors. A good example is smaller specialist food producers using online and other channels (such as farmers' markets) to 'bypass' the supermarkets to reach their target customers.

The marketer must be alert to channels changing over time. The growth in online channels is part of the reason for the recent decline in revenue experienced by UK high street retailers.

Summary

Today you learned that 'place' in the marketing mix is largely about channels of distribution – how a product/service is made available to the customer. Marketers can use intermediaries – retailers, wholesalers – if they add value to the marketing process, or they can trade directly with customers to reduce costs and increase the potential for building customer relations.

Direct channels can be broadly divided into traditional and new media. The recent significant growth of the Internet in terms of percentage share of the value of all UK retailing is one example of how different channels grow and decline over time.

Channels can have different characteristics. Some are exclusive relationships, like the dealer networks in the automotive market. Sometimes the intermediary can be the most powerful member of the distribution channel, as is the case with leading UK supermarkets.

Some organizations choose to be in the same channels as their competitors; others select channels offering a different route to their customers, such as direct marketing rather than retailers.

SUNDAY MONDAY TUESDAY WEDNESDAY THURSDAY FRIDAY SATURDAY

Fact-check (answers at the back)

1. What is a channel of distribution?
   a) Selling to Europe ❏
   b) Those third parties that make the product or service available for use or consumption by the customer ❏
   c) The spread of sales in different markets ❏
   d) None of the above ❏

2. Why must an intermediary like a retailer add value?
   a) Because of the common law of contract ❏
   b) They are only a service provider ❏
   c) They add cost so if they do not add value, there is no reason for a producer to use them ❏
   d) They are overrated ❏

3. Why are wholesalers different from retailers?
   a) They do not advertise ❏
   b) They sell to those buying for resale or business use ❏
   c) They have the highest sales volumes ❏
   d) All of the above ❏

4. What are two aspects of direct marketing?
   a) Traditional and new media ❏
   b) Profitable and non-profitable ❏
   c) Bulk based and individual units ❏
   d) Products and services ❏

5. Why is change over time important when considering channels?
   a) Because of seasonality ❏
   b) Because of the increasing cost of travelling ❏
   c) Over time different channels grow and then decline ❏
   d) Because of the lack of opportunities for out-of-town developments ❏

6. What does channel captaincy refer to?
   a) Taking the lead in developing a marketing campaign ❏
   b) Having control of shipping lines to Europe ❏
   c) The best retailers to use for products targeted at the leisure sailing market ❏
   d) Those members of the channel that have the most power ❏

7. Although channel members depend on one another, what do they often do?
   a) Act alone in their own short-term best interests ❏
   b) Misunderstand their roles ❏
   c) Fail to communicate with each other ❏
   d) Have different views about marketing ❏

8. What is the starting point for deciding a distribution strategy?
a) Who is available ❑
b) The production department ❑
c) Whether the channel puts the product where the customer wants to buy it ❑
d) Falling sales volumes ❑

9. Why do organizations often want to be in the same channel as their competitors?
a) They may be missing something ❑
b) Customers see their product at the same time they see their competitors' product ❑
c) They don't want to be left out ❑
d) It is what they have always done ❑

10. What dramatic increase in sales illustrates the growth of the Internet as a channel?
a) The BBC ❑
b) The Charities Commission ❑
c) Amazon.com ❑
d) Marmite ❑

SATURDAY

The marketing mix – promotion

Today we will look at the last of the 4 Ps of the marketing mix – *promotion*. This is the part of the mix that involves the organization in advancing and furthering its product or service in the minds of customers.

Promotion is also the most visible part of the marketing mix and can be seen alongside general entertainment on TV, radio and in the cinema and now increasingly on the Internet. It is understandable, therefore, that a large proportion of the general public perceives promotion to be synonymous with marketing. However, we know that promotion is only a *part* of marketing.

We will consider promotion in terms of marketing communications, the communication process, and the seven key decision areas of the promotional strategy. We will also discuss briefly ethics and regulation in this area.

Promotion and marketing communications

Promotion is the fourth part of the marketing mix and it can be thought of as the advancement or furtherance of a product or service in the mind of the customer. It is really about marketing communications and is concerned with **informing** and **persuading** customers.

Marketing communications involves developing and delivering co-ordinated messages designed to create a desired effect in a target audience. Ideally, marketing communications should manage the customer relationship over time, from the pre-purchase and purchase stages through to post-purchase and the brand's ongoing relationship with customers.

Communication is a process as depicted in the following model.

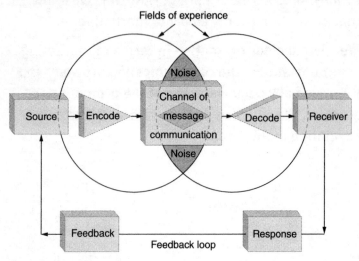

The communication process

The communication process involves ten elements.

1 **Source** – the organization sending the message to another party
2 **Encode** – the process of putting the intended message or thought into symbolic form, i.e. words and images

3 **Message** – the set of words, pictures or symbols that the source transmits
4 **Channel of communication** – the medium or media used by the source to carry the message to the receiver
5 **Decode** – the process by which the receiver assigns meaning to the message sent by the source
6 **Receiver** – the party receiving the message, normally the customer or potential customer but also including groups that may influence their opinions and behaviour
7 **Response** – the reactions of the receiver exposed to the message; this may be either a move from a state of unawareness of an offering to awareness or a move to a more committed position that will lead to a purchase
8 **Feedback** – the part of the receiver's response that is communicated back to the source, e.g. marketing research results
9 **Noise** – the unplanned 'static' or distortion during the communication process, which results in the receiver getting a different message from the one sent by the source. 'Static' could include competitors' messages, articles in magazines, blogs, etc.
10 **Fields of experience** – the more the source's and the receiver's fields of experience overlap, the more effective the message is likely to be.

Promotional strategy decisions

There are seven key decision areas involved in developing a promotional strategy.

1 Defining the target audience

On Wednesday we discussed the strategic process of defining which market segments the organization will target (the 'targeting' exercise). This exercise will have enabled us to define and profile the target customers in terms of both their perceived needs and their exposure to media. The organization may have multiple target segments and many of the following decision areas will be affected by their characteristics.

For example, younger target audiences can be difficult to reach using traditional media and the marketer would need to use new media (Internet and mobile-based).

2 Setting promotional objectives

While the ultimate objective is likely to be a purchase, promotional objectives will need to be drafted in terms of 'moving' the target audience towards this ultimate aim. Customers may move through a series of attitudinal stages – starting with **unawareness**, moving to **awareness**, developing an **understanding** of the benefits in the offering, and then becoming **convinced** that the offering meets their needs before taking **action** (purchasing). For instance, if the target audience is unaware of the organization's offering, the promotional objective is likely to be creating awareness. The marketer could therefore set an objective of 40 per cent of the target audience to be aware of the offering following the first stage of the campaign.

3 Creating the message(s)

The starting point for creating a message is an understanding of the task in hand. What are our promotional objectives? The message can be informative or persuasive, or both. A simple informative message may be 'Our new store opens on Monday at 8 a.m.' Persuasive messages form much of the media we all see and hear every day, in print, on television and radio, and on the Internet and mobile phones. These messages are developed by matching benefits to customers' perceived needs. Often marketers will seek to focus on the most important needs (from the hierarchy of needs discussed on Monday) as the basis for their messages.

To communicate this we need to 'encode' our message so that the customer will 'decode' it with maximum fidelity. It follows that the more we know about our target audience, the more effective our messages will be – marketing research at pre-campaign stage offers a valuable resource in this context. Message design can also be influenced by the nature of the medium. For instance, an advertisement in a magazine that could be re-read would be able to carry a more detailed message than a TV advertisement, but a TV advert would be able to use a range of moving images and sounds including music and dialogue.

4 Selecting the media

Media carry the message(s) to the target audiences and there are many media available to marketers.

- Advertising in print – includes national and regional newspapers, free press, special interest magazines (e.g. music, gardening), age-group targeted (e.g. *Saga Magazine*), lifestyle (e.g. *Tatler*)
- TV (terrestrial, cable and satellite) – carries sophisticated multimedia promotional messages
- Cinema – can run longer versions of TV adverts and can be targeted at audiences based on the nature of the film being shown
- Commercial radio – audio advertisements which, like cinema, can be targeted at particular groups based on the content of the programmes on air
- Personal selling – a very effective promotional medium because trained and experienced salespeople can interact with the customer; often a key part of B2B promotion and high-cost domestic durables, e.g. cars
- Direct marketing – postal, leaflet drop, telephone (including auto-dialling)
- Outdoor poster – includes large fixed billboards, bus stop, motorway, airport, underground, mobile (vehicle-based), inflatables
- Public relations – is the discipline which looks after reputation, with the aim of earning understanding and support and influencing opinion and behaviour. It is the planned and sustained effort to establish and maintain goodwill and mutual understanding between an organization and its public. Key to its success is the ability of the PR practitioner to place press releases in appropriate media
- Sponsorship – cash or in-kind support of anything from small regional events to major international events such as the Olympics and Football World Cup

- Online – from the proliferation of websites to sponsored links on search engines to specially designed adverts running on host sites including social networking sites such as Twitter and Facebook
- Mobile – the growth in ownership of smartphones and 3G/4G networks has given advertisers a new medium to deliver promotional messages to people's phones based on platforms including mobile browsers, apps (software applications) and SMS (short message service)

The marketer must select carefully. The first thing to consider is which media best 'reach' the target audience. By this we mean the number of people who will be exposed to the message carried by the medium. Clearly, the more of our target audience covered by the medium the better.

Secondly, the marketer must assess the relative cost of reaching an audience. Different media have different costs and reach, and marketers seek to create a reasonable comparison by dividing the cost of an advertisement in a particular medium by the reach (or coverage) of that medium, often expressed as a cost per 1,000 audience.

Thirdly, he/she will be interested in what the medium can 'do' for the message. Some media, such as exclusive magazines, can enhance the message by adding credibility to a product's advertisement.

5 Creating the promotional programme

The promotional programme has two components, the mix of media to be used and the schedule of activities over the time of the campaign. The following is an example of a simple programme.

Medium	Activity	Month 1	Month 2	Month 3	Month 4
TV	4 × 60 seconds	×		×	
Radio	6 × 20 seconds		×		×
Press	4 × 1/4 page	×		×	
Twitter	Weekly feed	×	×	×	×
Public relations	News releases	×		×	

The key thing for the marketer is to ensure an **integrated** programme of promotional activity that enables messages to build on earlier work and for themes to be **reinforced** as the campaign progresses. All too often, messages emanate from different parts of the organization with the result that the customer receives a mixed set, at worst contradictory, that can seriously reduce the effectiveness of the campaign.

6 Setting the budget

Setting the budget is often difficult. Some organizations base their decision on what they can afford. However, this method fails to link what needs to be done (the promotional objectives) with the resources to do it. Others use a percentage of sales approach, perhaps 10 per cent of last year's total sales made available for this year's promotional budget. Again, this method fails to link resources to objectives. Probably the best approach is the objective-and-task method – assessing what has to be achieved, the tasks involved and the estimated cost of performing these tasks.

7 Evaluating the results

Promotional spend is a business investment and therefore must be measured to assess its effectiveness. Unfortunately, it is difficult to measure the return on promotional spend (in sales and profit) because so many factors influence such measures. Effectiveness must therefore be measured in terms of meeting the promotional objectives through post-campaign research.

Ethics and regulation

In promoting a product or service it is particularly important that marketers maintain an ethical approach – that they do not use the promotional process to mislead customers. It may be tempting to make unsubstantiated claims to attract attention but, in addition to the fact that such action is immoral, it is bad for business and also illegal.

1 **Making unsubstantiated claims is bad for business**
  Although an organization might obtain a short-term advantage by misleading a customer, if the product or service does not satisfy customers' needs, they will not buy the product again. In addition, customers who feel badly treated by a supplier will tell their relations, friends and colleagues and this form of word-of-mouth communication is very powerful.

2 **Making unsubstantiated claims is illegal**
  Most developed economies legislate against bad promotional practice. In the UK the **Trade Descriptions Act 1968** prevents manufacturers, retailers and the service sector from misleading customers about what they are spending their money on. The Act empowers the courts to punish companies or individuals who make false claims.

  Each product sold must be '**as described**', of '**satisfactory quality**' and '**fit for purpose**'. 'As described' refers to any advertisement or verbal description made by the trader. 'Satisfactory quality' covers minor and cosmetic defects as well as substantial deficiencies and means that products must last a reasonable time. 'Fit for purpose' covers not only the obvious purpose of an item but also any purpose determined at the point of sale by the trader.

Independent regulators

The **Advertising Standards Authority (ASA)** is the UK's independent regulator of advertising, working to ensure that advertisements are **legal, decent, honest and truthful**. The US equivalent is the **Federal Trade Commission**. Their mission is to uphold standards in all media on behalf of consumers, business and society at large.

Summary

Today you learned that promotion is about marketing communications and is concerned with informing and persuading your target market. It is the most visible part of the marketing mix, appearing alongside entertainment on TV and radio, in the cinema and on the Internet.

Ideally, marketing communications should manage the customer relationship with the brand. At its root, communication involves encoding a message to be decoded by the receiver.

The seven key decision areas involved in developing a promotional strategy are: defining the audience; setting objectives; creating the message(s); selecting the media; creating the programme; setting the budget; and evaluating the results.

When promoting a product/service, marketers must not use the promotional process to mislead customers. Legislation and regulation exist to protect customers, but it is the responsibility of professional marketers to act ethically and not to make unsubstantiated claims.

SUNDAY
MONDAY
TUESDAY
WEDNESDAY
THURSDAY
FRIDAY
SATURDAY

Fact-check (answers at the back)

1. What is the promotion part of the marketing mix?
   a) Marketing communications ❑
   b) The 'glossy' part ❑
   c) All about TV ❑
   d) Not important to the success of the business ❑

2. Why does a large proportion of the general public perceive promotion to be synonymous with marketing?
   a) Advertising *is* marketing ❑
   b) Promotion is the most visible part of the marketing mix ❑
   c) It's part of the entertainment business ❑
   d) All of the above ❑

3. What does the heart of the communication process involve?
   a) Closing the sale ❑
   b) Getting the best price for printed materials ❑
   c) The source encoding a message to be decoded by the receiver ❑
   d) Subliminal messages ❑

4. How must promotional objectives be set?
   a) In terms of moving the audience through a series of attitudinal stages to the purchase stage ❑
   b) In terms of sales ❑
   c) According to the time of the year ❑
   d) According to the number of specialist sales staff available ❑

5. What can messages be?
   a) Read or heard ❑
   b) Seen or viewed ❑
   c) Informative and/or persuasive ❑
   d) None of the above ❑

6. What is media reach?
   a) The number of people in an audience that will be exposed to the message carried by the medium ❑
   b) The reputation of a newspaper or TV channel ❑
   c) The amount a customer must pay to access a medium ❑
   d) Always much higher than the medium claims ❑

7. What are the two components of creating a promotional programme?
   a) The mix of media to be used and the schedule of activities over the time of the campaign ❑
   b) Sales staff and marketing staff ❑
   c) Time of year and product type ❑
   d) Retailer and competitor activity ❑

8. Why is it difficult to measure the financial return, such as sales or profit, on promotional spend?
   a) Because of the way costs are accounted for ❑
   b) Seasonal factors need to be taken into account ❑
   c) So many factors additional to the promotional activities influence such measures ❑
   d) Because of differences in retailers' sales systems ❑

9. Why may it be tempting to make an unsubstantiated claim?
a) To attract attention ❏
b) To mislead the competition ❏
c) To get the campaign under way quickly ❏
d) To make the shareholders happy ❏

10. In addition to regulation, for what reason must the professional marketer guard against making unsubstantiated claims?
a) It's bad for business ❏
b) Because of competitors' reactions ❏
c) Because of retailers' reactions ❏
d) None of the above ❏

SUNDAY
MONDAY
TUESDAY
WEDNESDAY
THURSDAY
FRIDAY
SATURDAY

Surviving in tough times

No business is immune from the significant changes now occurring in the economic environment. What's going to happen? What should we do? To a certain extent, it's anyone's guess. What we can be sure of is that many sectors will see shrinking demand, which is likely to increase the competitive pressures facing businesses. Under these conditions a business must redouble its focus on two key groups – customers and competitors. Here are ten crucial tips you can use to help your business survive and prosper.

1 Focus on your customers

During difficult times, customers may be changing in terms of their perceived needs, buying habits and attitudes to value. Marketers must not assume they *know* what customers are thinking. Use current research to ensure that you have an objective view of the situation. Having up-to-date information on customers will help you identify the right course of action to meet corporate objectives in a changing environment.

2 Focus on your competitors

Businesses will generally adopt three broad approaches during difficult trading conditions. Most commonly, they reduce their prices to stimulate their own customers' demand and to attract competitors' customers. Alternatively, they will increase the benefits they offer while keeping prices steady (e.g. 2-for-1 offers or free trial periods). Firms may also create innovative solutions to customers' perceived needs. The marketer must ensure that information on competitor action is collected and used as part of the strategic decision process. The key is to take the right action at the right time based on sound research.

3 Know yourself

We have seen the need for a business audit as part of the marketing planning process, and during difficult times businesses must be especially alert to their own strengths and weaknesses. The key issue is to be *objective* – too many businesses flatter themselves regarding their strengths and underestimate their weaknesses. During tough times, being honest with oneself provides a sound basis for dealing with change. It is documented that managers can be 'myopic', i.e. fail to see how changes in demand can affect their products. We must guard against this problem.

4 Get your segmentation right

Is your segmentation right for the current circumstances? Your customers may be changing and these changes are likely to create new market segments. Parts of one segment may now be more or less attractive to your business (e.g. customers' disposable income may not be as adversely affected as others' in the segment) and the business has to respond to such changes. Current marketing research is critical to produce up-to-date information, and you have to be able to act on this information to target redefined market segments. Failure to do this may have a marked effect on business success.

5 Enhance responsiveness and flexibility

These two interrelated qualities are of particular value to a business during difficult economic conditions. You may have up-to-date information about your customers and competitors but, unless you are willing to be responsive to change and flexible in your approach, obtaining such information is just an arid academic exercise. One of the main threats for any manager during such times is inertia – simply carrying on as before – but if we do this we will be at a competitive disadvantage.

6 Know your products' benefits

To facilitate an 'exchange', products and services must carry benefits that match the perceived needs of the customer. When economic times are tough, customers are more likely to review their buying decisions and look at alternative ways of meeting their perceived needs. This presents businesses with both a threat (to their current customer base) and an opportunity (where competitors' customers may now be interested in our offerings). Again, we need up-to-date information to ensure that we select the right strategic responses to the current situation.

7 Understand pricing and value

Customers become more price sensitive during difficult economic conditions, and will shop around for the same products at a lower cost. Customers may even 'brand switch', buying an alternative, cheaper brand from their usual purchase. In a 'price-dominant' decision the customer will simply buy the cheapest product, regardless of differences in benefits; in a 'best-value' decision the customer weighs up the benefits and cost of each offering and looks for the best value, i.e. the most benefits at the lowest cost. Marketers must know how their customers are thinking about price and value.

8 Get promotion right

Communicating with the market is important at any time, but marketers need to be flexible and adaptable when planning their promotional strategies. The marketer has to be ready to change messages and media to respond to customers' needs and competitor actions. Short-term campaigns are required to enable the business to redirect resources as required.

9 Act quickly

We have extolled the virtues of the ancient Greek proverb, 'Think slowly, act quickly', and this is particularly relevant during difficult economic conditions. You have less time available to plan and the consequences of making a wrong decision are more acute, but failure to act will ultimately put the business at a competitive disadvantage. Marketers have to use information to reduce risk in decision making but must not be paralysed into inaction through lack of 'perfect' information. We can only reduce risk; there is always an element of risk, but inaction places our destiny in the hands of others.

10 Monitor and control outcomes

All good planning systems link outcomes to the set objectives and during tough times this is paramount. The time frame for monitoring outcomes and objectives – e.g. the effects of price changes or promotional messages – often becomes much shorter, and needs to be assessed in months rather than years. Strategies must then be revised in the light of new information. Some of the factors driving the difficult environment are outside the control of the business but must be understood by the business, so assess the probability of different PEST conditions prevailing and consider your responses to these conditions.

Answers

Sunday: 1a; 2c; 3b; 4b; 5c; 6a; 7b; 8b; 9c; 10d.

Monday: 1b; 2a; 3b; 4a; 5d; 6a; 7d; 8b; 9d; 10d.

Tuesday: 1a; 2b; 3b; 4a; 5b; 6a; 7b; 8b; 9d; 10c.

Wednesday: 1a; 2c; 3b; 4a; 5a; 6b; 7a; 8d; 9a; 10d.

Thursday: 1d; 2c; 3b; 4d; 5a; 6a; 7d; 8c; 9d; 10b.

Friday: 1b; 2c; 3b; 4a; 5c; 6d; 7a; 8c; 9b; 10c.

Saturday: 1a; 2b; 3c; 4a; 5c; 6a; 7a; 8c; 9a; 10a.